THE INNER TAROT

THE inner TAROT

A Modern Approach to Self-Compassion
& Empowered Healing Using the Tarot

KATE VAN HORN

sounds true
BOULDER, COLORADO

Sounds True
Boulder, CO

Published 2024

Cover design by Michelle Azzi and Lisa Kerans
Book design by Rachael Murray

Illustrations from the Rider-Waite Tarot Deck® reproduced by permission of U.S.
Games Systems, Inc., Stamford, CT 06902 USA. Copyright ©1971 by U.S.
Games Systems, Inc. Further reproduction prohibited. The Rider-Waite Tarot
Deck® is a registered trademark of U.S. Games Systems, Inc.

Printed in the United States of America

BK06904

Library of Congress Cataloging-in-Publication Data

Names: Van Horn, Kate, author.
Title: The inner tarot : a modern approach to self-compassion & empowered
healing using the tarot / Kate Van Horn.
Description: Boulder, CO : Sounds True, 2024.
Identifiers: LCCN 2023026968 (print) | LCCN 2023026969 (ebook) |
    ISBN 9781649632487 (paperback) | ISBN 9781649632494 (ebook)
Subjects: LCSH: Tarot.
Classification: LCC BF1879.T2 V354 2024 (print) | LCC
BF1879.T2 (ebook) |
    DDC 133.3/2424--dc23/eng/20230606
LC record available at https://lccn.loc.gov/2023026968
LC ebook record available at https://lccn.loc.gov/2023026969

If I have ever read your cards, this book is dedicated to you.

Contents

Introduction

When I tell people I'm a professional tarot reader and psychic, I get looks of shock followed by immediate intrigue. I get flooded with questions (which I never get tired of answering, by the way) that range from, "Did you know you had that gift growing up?" to, "Is it overwhelming to be a psychic?" to, "So do you, like, see ghosts and stuff?" The answer to all those questions, plainly, is no. I understand their curiosities and assumptions—I've seen *Bewitched* and *That's So Raven* after all—but my spiritual awakening and initiation into this work looked quite different than you probably expect.

I like to let people in on the truth right away, which is that I was an anxious child but not necessarily an intuitive child. I am a psychic, but I know when and how to turn the gifts "off" and be a regular ol' human being. And I've spoken to a ghost or two, but don't worry, they're harmless. That's a topic for another day (or book). Truthfully, I had no idea that my hypersensitivities were related to intuition, much less that they would later become the focus of my work and what I passionately share with a global community.

I believe my history, experiences, and traumas slowly and subtly guided me toward a psychic awakening and reconnection. I never had an immediate *knowing* or epiphany. Tarot became one of many tools in my personal healing toolkit that helped me piece together the parts that I perceived as broken, the same parts of me that I now celebrate and show off. My tarot experience began a decade ago, and I plan on sharing plenty more about my relationship with these cards throughout this book.

But before giving tarot readings to others, I studied and practiced it personally. By looking deeply at the theme of each card, relating it to my experiences and integrating their teachings, I began to feel more and more whole. I was in love with the cards almost instantly, and eventually I entered into this profession in order to help others to not only understand the cards and their traditional meanings, but also to learn to trust this tool as they tap into their intuition, prioritize their inner healing, and connect through personal storytelling.

I'm quite good at reading cards, and I've become damn proud of this skill I've honed. I credit my intuitive gifts, of course, but also recognize how important my commitment and dedication to the practice are. I've worked on my relationship with the cards each and every day since I purchased my first deck, and I strive to always bring integrity to my readings.

I vividly remember the time in therapy when I said something to my therapist that was so candid that it startled and saddened me at the same time. I told her the only things I could really do well were self-sabotage and live in fear of my own power. There was nothing I could name that I felt naturally gifted or good at. I later wrote about the realization in my channeled writing and personal journaling:

> My body fragile,
> And my faith clearly faltering,
> I remember, clear as day, sitting on the
> couch in my therapist's office.
> "Why are you holding on to behaviors that hurt you?"
> "Because being this way, acting this way, is
> the one thing I'm good at."
> I thank God every day that I was wrong about that.

Today, at a very different stage of my life, I'm overwhelmed with not only gratitude for the opportunity to call this my job, but also with satisfaction and a deep sense of relief. My hardships are what led me here. At this point in my professional career as an intuitive,

I've taught thousands of tarot enthusiasts how to read cards through my courses and trainings. I've also read for thousands of clients one-on-one, holding space and sharing spiritual guidance in a grounded and relatable way. I've amassed a large social media following spanning multiple platforms, where I teach the cards' symbolism and details of this revered and ancient system. I've hosted numerous psychic retreats, gathered souls in countless healing circles, and shared many pieces of spiritual content and writing along the years—almost too many to count. I've spent a great deal of time and commitment developing my knowledge of these cards, similar to the time spent healing and keeping the commitments I made to myself.

Beyond these successes though, I want to specify that my community and our experience together is not back-alley magic. It's not cheesy or hokey in any way. The way I teach these cards isn't based on clickbait or reliant on dramatic claims about anyone's future or fate. Instead, we, as a collective, embrace the true inner work together, and boy, is it beautiful. Moving through topics and truths that others might shy away from, we speak and share freely. We've built a container of support that is never judgmental, never shameful, and never *ever* unsafe. It's the space my inner child has always craved.

I promise each member of my community that I will uphold what I originally intended with this work: to share psychic practices with spiritual safety and encourage unapologetic growth and evolution. Spiritual leadership brings great responsibility, and I make sure to embody the same authenticity I ask of each client who bravely sits within the spaces, readings, and groups I facilitate. If you're holding this book, I want you to consider yourself a part of this community too.

Through this guidebook, you'll learn that the tarot deck is broken into two main parts: the Major Arcana and the Minor Arcana. The word *Arcana*, from the Latin *arcanus*, translates to "secrets." I think it's so fascinating that the tarot deck is quite literally full of secrets—a total of seventy-eight, in fact. Some are small and incremental, revolving around our everyday experiences (Minor Arcana), and some are monumental and profoundly difficult to share (Major Arcana). All of the themes are crucial for us to uncover so that we might more clearly understand all parts of our identity and our greater purpose.

I think the secretive nature of tarot is exactly what captivates us in the first place. It's the reason I get those bewildered looks and questions when I share my profession. These cards create a stack of unknown information that we long to decipher, and their messages are available through a practice that's alluring and slightly taboo, even. Some people might typecast a tarot reader as a crazy aunt who has a shelf full of decks and burns a lot of incense, but as we mature and grow less judgmental, we might realize she was onto something when it comes to expressing our intuition—and that this aunt wasn't so crazy after all!

It's through their sense of mystery that the cards draw us in. They faintly whisper invitations, tempting us with their wisdom. They're mesmerizing to us, not because they differ from the typical search engines we rely on for answers, but because they serve as mirrors, reflecting all our facets and flaws and offering an opportunity to discover the answers hidden within us all along.

The mysticism, secrecy, and assumed darkness in the practice of tarot made me feel incredibly seen. I think this is because at the time I discovered the cards, I related to secrecy and shadow and was working to uncover and reveal parts of myself that I hadn't yet brought to light. I enjoyed the way the cards called me out on obvious struggles rather than circumventing them or bypassing the truth of what I really was facing.

Growing up, I held a lot of my own secrets. I kept secrets about what was happening in my home, what was happening to my body, and how much shame I felt. In my early twenties, I was diagnosed with PTSD, which was simultaneously devastating and freeing. My diagnosis came after a series of difficult years, where my emotions ran high and my faith in myself wore thin. And it only came to light after I shared a secret that I had kept locked away for close to fifteen years.

By sharing the truth, the floodgates of old memories, feelings, and energies reopened, and perhaps my third eye did as well, although I wasn't aware of it then. I had been in survival mode for so long, but receiving the label of PTSD didn't feel limiting. Instead, it felt incredibly validating. It gave me a chance to redefine myself. I could now respond to this information on my own terms; putting language to my condition became the catalyst and benchmark for me to change the course of my life, discover and express my intuition, and stop shrinking and hiding myself.

Before I continue, I'd like to offer a trigger warning: I'm about to share a story of childhood sexual abuse. This was the first secret cast on my story, and I now understand that it led me toward a path to discover my inner light and divine purpose. It saddens me to know that a not-so-small number of readers will feel their own bodies react to my story. Their stomachs might plummet or churn with a familiar-but-furious relatability, thinking to themselves, *Oh, that happened to her, too.*

The day I lost touch with my body was the day I was first sexually abused as a child. I became immediately frozen and shut down—a changed version of myself. I was a tiny human experiencing big traumas. At the time, those experiences conditioned me to believe my pain was not important, that those parts of me were something to never be shared or exposed. I was unknowingly committed to a lifelong journey to regain safety and trust in my own home and my most sacred of spaces: my body, my life, my *self.*

Even when the abuse ended, my spirit held an imprint of its darkness. Over time, my connection to myself felt inconsistent and even confusing. I wasn't sure who I could really be or what I truly wanted. Most of my time was spent avoiding or denying feelings of fear, rather than thriving or discovering what I could be led to next. This disconnection with myself manifested in a number of ways, from depression and disordered eating to reactivity and intense anger. Now that I've learned more about trauma survivors and our responses, I hold more empathy for myself. The chaos I created is a common defense mechanism.

During my teens and young adult years, I was consistently on edge, angry, and, dare I say, bitchy. I didn't realize my inner child was kicking and screaming for my attention, creating an uproar anytime the circumstances made her feel threatened. She was asking me to share the secret so she could finally move forward.

My memories of childhood were often blank, and as I grew older my panic attacks started to creep in during the strangest of circumstances, like in classrooms or movie theaters, leaving me to feel out of control. The fear of feeling my own fear manifested into more fears, and by the time I was a teenager, I felt limited. I had no idea what I was capable of, what I was strong enough to do, who I wanted to become. My nerves ran on high alert. I was hypervigilant, and my distrust of others presented itself in a variety of chaotic social responses, mean-girl tendencies, and disrespect for my body. I chose to disrespect myself first before I could ever become a "victim" again. This self-sabotage took form in various ways, through an eating disorder and by seeking out validation from men. My behaviors hindered my relationships, my confidence, and my sense of purpose. What I understand now is that my big secret as a child initiated a domino effect, tumbling me down a path toward true self-discovery. As an adult, I now realize it is my responsibility to stand each fallen domino right back up, like sturdy and resilient soldiers, committing to taking up space and sharing my stories in the ways I always deserved to.

Around the time of my PTSD diagnosis, my healing became a focus because it had to be. My anxiety was debilitating, and I was beginning to lose hope in the idea that I could eventually grow into an adult who was capable of holding a steady job or connecting with a loving and healthy partner. For the next few years, it felt like my full-time job was healing and deconditioning the old and traumatized parts of me while reconnecting with a version of myself that felt somewhat familiar and somewhat like a stranger.

I worked on healing in clinical settings at first. There were no crystal balls or fun intuitive tools (yet). Name a therapy technique or resource, and I bet I've tried it. I experienced everything, from intensive and specialized treatment programs to group therapy, EMDR, medication, and eventually yoga, journaling, and prayer. My therapists saved me from settling for a narrative I didn't want to commit to, but I still craved softer modalities that felt more supportive and hopeful. Through my search for more spiritually centered tools, I eventually picked up a deck of tarot cards. They felt feminine, welcoming, and fascinating to me. They showed me that my many facets and flaws were beautiful and unique. Each time I committed to my tarot practice, I was committed to my inner healing. This ritual became the vehicle I could steer through my journey back to my authenticity. The memories and moments I was once ashamed of had an opportunity to be rewritten over each card I reflected on, and these stories became pillars, benchmarks, and milestones that marked chapters I could take pride in.

Since beginning my healing journey, I've become fascinated by the stories of others and the way our resilience can carry us up and through the depths of just about any obstacle. Sitting across from someone over the cards is one of the most intimate and sacred experiences you can have, in my opinion. It's why I never tire of tarot and sharing readings. I get to listen, attentive and in awe, hearing the ways my clients have handled adversity so gracefully and how we all brave the challenging ebbs and flows of life, looking for meaning and belonging in the process of healing.

But sometimes when someone is sharing themselves or being "read" quite literally by me, I watch them start to retract, wondering if they should keep some of what is coming up in the reading stifled down and not admit to some of the shadows or imperfections the cards are illuminating.

Through this book, I propose that we reframe and redefine the secrets we hold within. I'd like us to celebrate our narratives by changing how we view and speak of our scars. Let's make an adjustment to the verbiage and tone we attach to them. Rather than seeing the not-so-pretty parts of our stories as something to hide, let's allow these cards and their messages to help us embrace them. Consider them an invitation inward or a chance to wander back home to yourself.

Within these pages you'll read about the discoveries I made about myself through my inner work, as well as the areas I'm continuing to heal today. My goal is to position tarot and the ritual of pulling cards in such a way that your secrets begin to feel sacred, like spaces to uncover and areas to celebrate and discover, rather than something shameful.

How to Learn Through This Book

The Inner Tarot will not only serve as your resource for reading cards, but also as a new access point into your inner work. This book will encourage you to recall your memories, share the messiest parts of yourself, and explore your truths so others can appreciate *all* of you as you honor yourself. I'll offer practices, suggestions, and examples of how to do this.

I encourage you to take what resonates and release anything that doesn't. Throughout my healing I went through much trial and error. I found spaces and tools that worked well for me and felt authentic, as well as others that fascinated me but just felt forced. The same could ring true in the offerings I share here. Some cards will feel like an instant friend, and others you'll resist, like a foe. I recommend you remove your judgment of what tarot needs to look like or if you're doing it *well*, and instead focus most on authenticity and sustainability.

In Part 1 we'll explore the nuances of pulling cards to ground you in the practice and give you the tools to become a confident reader. Consider it a crash course in card reading. I'll share my tips for creating rituals around your deck, understanding numerology, reading reversals, crafting tarot spreads, and more.

Part 2 is what you'll refer to again and again as you create your tarot practice and routines. Beginning with the Minor Arcana, we'll explore all fourteen cards of each suit then follow with the beautiful and symbolically rich Major Arcana. I'll offer quick keywords for easy reference as well as more dense definitions for deeper study. We'll complete the learning of each card with two tangible practices for integration and reflection. These practices are created with the intention to drop you further into your tarot experience, making card themes more memorable and personal as you embody them. Expect lots of journal prompts throughout this book. I believe writing and tarot are symbiotic partners, so I recommend dedicating a journal exclusively to reflecting on your card pulls! I've also provided somatic practices and practical tools you can use to work with the energy each card is presenting.

Perhaps the most intimate and vulnerable aspect of this book is my channeled writing paired with each tarot card. These are words I've written throughout my own inner healing journey as I discovered myself in new ways, with a deck of cards dancing in my hands and a pen to my journal. These are more of my secrets, matched with the specific card that reminded me to release any shame around it. This personal poetry is the fullest expression of myself, and I'm honored to share it with you.

I hope you can feel my love for the process and for the cards themselves, and I hope you are able to notice the way my story mirrors or reminds you of chapters of your own.

Now, let's head inward.

Part 1

1

In Review

THE HISTORY OF TAROT

Tarot wasn't always used for divination. In fact, it's not quite as ancient or magical of a tool as people might expect. Although we now use the cards as a resource to help aid our self-inquiry and get to know Spirit a bit better, in their original form, they were never intended to be used for healing or fortune-telling purposes at all. While they certainly have evolved to carry a stigma of mysticism and associations with witches and psychics, the history of tarot is much simpler: it originated in the north of Italy around the 1400s as a game[1] . . .

. . . and that's it. Tarot cards were not awe-inspiring, not ominous, they were just a game.

Their story and purpose have obviously grown more complex over time, but their first application was to provide entertainment to nobility. The game they would play using these cards was called *tarocchi*.[2] Right around the same time that illuminated manuscripts were in vogue, wealthy Italian families would commission beautifully illustrated, often gilded, decks from notable local artists. These decks were called *carte da trionfi*, which is loosely translated as "triumph cards."[3] (We'll talk more about this in the next chapter, but the cards in the Major Arcana are sometimes called "Trump Cards" in reference to this.)

What we now know as the fourteen-card Minor Arcana suits was a collection of "pip cards," which consisted of ten numbered cards and anywhere between three and six male court cards.[4] The suits we have now very much echo the ones from back then, although the Pentacles suit was sometimes referred to as the Coins or Disks suit, and the Suit of Wands was sometimes known as the Suit of Batons, Sticks, Staves, or Rods.[5]

Just like our modern decks, the images on the cards represented themes we encounter along our journeys. They are reflective of what we experience in our day-to-day lives, showing triumphs and tribulations common in every community. Visual representation of elements from Jewish, Egyptian, and Christian ideologies, as well as astrology, are prominent throughout the imagery.[6] Everything from the Torah in The High Priestess card to the twelve stars, representing the zodiac, on The Empress's crown indicates how many creeds have influenced our modern decks. Although the numbers of some cards are switched in certain decks (Justice and Strength), and others have characters like Popes and Knaves and Lust, their purpose is the same: to reflect the human experience.[7]

Eventually, the variety of themes represented in the cards birthed another game called *tarocchi appropriati*. Players—those noble Italians I mentioned before—would write poems about one another inspired by the themes the cards represented.[8] I adore this because it's essentially a version of the channeled writing I'll ask you to do later in this book. The game was a primitive form of reading for one another.

But it wasn't until a few hundred years later, around 1800, that *tarocchi* emerged in France as *tarot* as we know it today.[9] In 1909, British mystic Arthur Edward Waite published a deck with the Rider Company. It was illustrated by Pamela Colman Smith, a female artist from London who identified as an occultist. Pamela was an acquaintance of Waite, as they were both members of the same secret society.[10] Before her interpretations, the Minor Arcana was represented more simply, with one coin on the Ace of Pentacles, two coins on the Two of Pentacles, and so on.

Smith was the first to illustrate the full story of the Minor Arcana with rich colors and expressive characters, and she marked each card with her serpentine signature.[11] She modernized the deck, to tell the full story. This version, and its art, remains the most produced and commonly referenced tarot deck to date.[12]

I believe Smith had a natural ability to give these cards such personality and depth. I like to think she channeled this art. The frustrating part is, for a long time she was never given proper credit for her passionate work. There was a time when her name wasn't mentioned in the deck title at all, despite the fact that tarot is a visual practice and one would assume the artist would be praised.[13] She changed the system altogether, so you'll read Rider-Waite-Smith instead of just Rider-Waite throughout this book in my descriptions and references of this deck. I encourage you to channel your inner Smith and study your cards with a keen eye. You never know what you might find hidden in her illustrations that resonates with you.

So why is this history important to know as you move forward? First, to honor a practice that has evolved and transformed greatly over time, much like you. Second, I hope this understanding of their history helps to demystify them a bit, and leads you to have a healthier relationship with them. I've noticed over my years of reading that people can become reliant on the cards, turning to them in moments of crisis (I'll talk more about what I call "panic pulling" later). They expect their decks to offer solutions to important questions or act as erasers for past difficulties. However, that was never their original intent, and the goal of this book is to appreciate their stories as they mirror your personal experiences.

Whenever you start to feel anxious about a "negative" card showing up in a reading, I hope you're able to offer yourself a reframe. Whatever the cards are bringing you is not law. In fact, the cards are just cards; it's our relationship with them that's sacred, not the pieces of paper themselves. (In fact, I am so unattached to my decks that I actually enjoy burning an occasional card and take pride when one slips out of its deck to be lost in the ether.) The cards are not telling us anything specific; they are merely a vessel through which Spirit can send us messages.

Every reader will have different ways of interpreting them, and at the end of the day, you have free will. *Use it!*

Myth Busting

Once I clear the air after my psychic abilities and relationship with the cards are called into question, people often ask me about how they can establish their own relationship with their deck. I recognize that even though I've become incredibly comfortable with them, and reading is now second nature to me, for someone who is new to this it can feel like opening Pandora's box.

Tarot faces its fair share of stigmas, and any questions you might have about the practice are warranted. When you begin reading cards, you enter uncharted territory. Just like The Fool, an exciting journey awaits you. The fewer expectations or stereotypes you carry into the practice, the more you can choose your own adventure. Go ahead and ask your questions, but do your due diligence first! There are quite a few myths about tarot I've had to debunk along the way, and I'll encourage you to stay just as open-minded and let yourself learn new truths about these cards.

Do the cards hold a "magic" I should fear?

Depending on your experience and history with spirituality, religion, and intuition, tarot might feel like some sort of malevolent "magic." Society has labeled a lot of feminine practices as wrong, but I promise you that you're not sinning or communing with the devil if you pull tarot cards. In fact, it's quite the opposite. The more you work with them as a healing modality, the more light they hold! Tarot is a powerful practice. If you approach it with love, it will love you right back.

Do I need to be psychic to read tarot?

No. But tarot is one of the best entry points into psychic exploration, if you want it to be. More than anything, it's a way to prompt discussion with yourself. The card themes are so authentic, profound, and challenging that inevitably we access parts of ourselves that are less logical and more raw when we start pulling. Your intuition can naturally start to come into play without you even knowing because you're having a different inner dialogue, taking yourself out of autopilot to tap into something more sacred.

Will tarot tell me my future?

Like most things in life, the answer is both yes and no. Tarot is all about reading the energy of the present. We can see an energetic forecast in the cards we pull based on what's happening in real time and what we're asking of them. Then, we can make actionable changes, utilize our free will, and intervene with purpose to realign and match ourselves with different destinies.

If you feel in touch with your witchy side, and divination is something you feel intrigued by and consider safe to explore, then please go for it; there is a fortune-telling side of tarot available. But don't feel like you have to predict anything with these cards if it feels forced or unnatural to channel. Know that you can just pull for practice and reflection. Tarot can always stay in the present for you.

Do I need to be gifted my first tarot deck?

No. This is merely a superstition. I do think it's beautiful when anyone gives you a meaningful gift that's meant to be so personal (beats another candle or bottle of wine, right?). However, my favorite decks are the ones I bought myself whenever I felt drawn to them. This practice is meant to be empowering, so if you feel an urge to buy a deck, listen to the call!

Are there good cards and bad cards?

There are cards that are easier to sit with, ones we want to relish in longer, and cards we want to heal ourselves out of immediately. It's just like life! All the experiences we'll ever have are neutral; we're the ones who assign them emotions and choose how we respond to them. It's normal for us to want to lean toward situations or pull away from others.

There is neutrality, shadow, and light in every card. Difficult cards, like The Tower or The Devil, have their silver linings. Cards we view more positively, like The Sun and Strength, can be taken to the extreme. Living in binary is not fun, and I challenge you to resist the urge to label any of these cards on one end of the spectrum or the other. We don't typically pick up an intuitive practice to live by even more rules, regulations, and expectations, so why bring that stuffiness and formality to the beauty of our connection with tarot? I believe there is no need for such labels in spiritual work.

Does tarot have to be an independent practice?
I recommend prioritizing your private conversations with your tarot deck. It can be a beautiful experience to allow the cards to serve as a conduit between you and Spirit. But humans, particularly women, have gathered together for generations, and there's something special about using this tool as a team as well.

We are community-based beings. We thrive in our ability to share and tell stories together. My healing wouldn't have been possible without my community. This book will help us all recall the fact that tarot used to be a social practice.[14] I've tried my best to detail how you can share the lessons of the cards with others and experience a deeper connection to them yourself. Talk about your learnings and freely share your experience with those you love and those who are curious but hesitant to begin. If you're proud, introduce them to your cards and share your new knowledge!

2

In Parts

There is a clear and thoughtful system in tarot, so let's differentiate and define each piece of this tool in parts. By understanding the basic structure of the deck and its system, we can ground ourselves as readers and see how they are not randomly placed, but instead outline a cohesive story. We will first meet our protagonist (The Fool) numbered at zero and follow and transform alongside them for the remaining seventy-seven cards. With so much nuance and detail in each of these individual themes, the outline and structure that tarot follows naturally helps us, as readers, compartmentalize where we can focus our attention and what we might expect along the way.

There are seventy-eight cards (and no fewer).
A traditional tarot deck consists of seventy-eight cards, and no fewer. All seventy-eight cards have been placed intentionally into an organized system to tell a story that builds upon itself in meaning and complexity. I am a firm believer that a standard deck must be seventy-eight cards to pay respect to the traditional meanings and the practice

of reading tarot. There are adaptations with additional cards that have been added by various artists and authors, which is a fun way to show creative liberty and add some supporting themes, but the majority of the decks you will come across hold exactly seventy-eight meanings across the Major Arcana and Minor Arcana.

You might discover a deck you resonate with that has fewer than seventy-eight cards. These decks will likely be oracle cards, affirmation cards, or angel cards, and while they can absolutely be powerful healing tools and inspiring to work with, they shouldn't be compared to traditional tarot decks.

The Major Arcana

The Major Arcana consists of twenty-two cards, starting with The Fool (at 0, or unnumbered) and ending with The World (21). These cards represent the soul's experience and our spiritual growth. They are more archetypal and thematic than the Minor Arcana because they represent the larger universal energy (and adversity) we face throughout our lives. The Major Arcana cards, sometimes referred to as Trump cards, are memorable because they represent powerful chapters in our lives. They bring us messages and indicate periods of change, death, rebirth, and union.

I affectionately label these cards the "heavy hitters" of the tarot deck because their themes are dense in symbolism and intention. The Major Arcana holds monumental weight over our healing experiences, so when you're reading cards from this section of the deck, give them special attention and consider them as anchors to your reading. They are sharing the key lessons and most prominent energy that you have access to at the time you're pulling cards.

The Minor Arcana

The Minor Arcana consists of fifty-six cards across four suits, similar to a deck of playing cards. Each suit carries ten numbered cards (Ace through Ten) plus four court cards.

The Minor Arcana is the larger portion of the deck and represents our day-to-day lifestyle, tasks, relationships, and experiences. It feels more familiar and perhaps redundant because these are energies we work with frequently, or repeatedly, throughout our life cycle. Diverse in energy, the Minor Arcana offers insight and direction on how to act on, respond to, and integrate the lessons and spiritual growth of the Major Arcana.

Pentacles/Earth: The Pentacles suit relates to anything in the material world. This includes our physical body and health, our home, our finances, and our career. Earth is the element associated with this suit and cycle. It is practical, hardworking, loyal, and patient.

Cups/Water: The Cups suit follows our emotional realm. It relates to our many emotions, all types of relationships, and our subconscious mind. Water is the associated element, which relates to healing, vulnerability, and sensitivity. These cards can also emphasize our intuitive connection and empathy.

Swords/Air: The Swords suit rules our intellect and mind. It connects our thoughts, our communication (verbal and nonverbal), our intelligence, and our logic. Air is the associated element, which makes this energy adaptable, quick-moving, and curious. These cards can also relate to our personal truth, authenticity, and integrity, as they value justice, fairness, and honesty.

Wands/Fire: The Wands suit is connected to our personal power, our passions, and our confidence. It investigates our relationship with and awareness of our purpose, our creative vision, and our primal instincts. Associated with the fire element, it's intense and transformative. This element taps us into our ego and reacts to conflict or inspiration quickly. The Wands suit is the change-making area of the deck, full of magic and individuality.

Court Cards
The court cards make up the final four cards in each Minor Arcana suit. Across the four suits, these court cards create sixteen personality types

and mini "families" within the Tarot. Each court consists of a king, a queen, a knight, and a page.

Court Card Representations

Ourselves: Especially when you're pulling cards for yourself, court cards are likely referencing some area of your personality that you should lean into, appreciate, and depend on more to overcome whatever conflict or challenges are present. Alternatively, the tarot could be illuminating a space in your personality that could be released or matured, a space for you to evolve.

Some questions you can ask yourself after you pull a court card:

- Does this court card personality sound like how my friends and family would describe me?
- What gifts does this personality have that I also see in myself?
- Does this card reflect a part of my personality I'm proud of?
- Am I sharing these parts of myself confidently?

Other people: Sometimes court cards represent your partner, best friend, toxic co-worker, mother, or sibling. Use your intuitive knowing here and go with your gut! Sometimes you'll feel confident that the personality represents someone else in your life. The deck could be showing a person you can count on to help you, a relationship dynamic that needs a boundary, or a past lover who is still taking up space in your energetic awareness and needs to be released through more healing. Notice the gifts and strengths as well as the shadows of these personalities. How are their traits matching and supporting you, and how are they hindering your self-connection and balance?

Events and/or news: Although we are typically reading these cards as characters in our story, occasionally they will arrive to mark an event, represent incoming news, or reflect the development and maturation of energy. The knights and kings can be associated with events. The pages carry news and messages for us, and the queens can represent the birth of a creative project or new opportunity.

Court Card Rank and Maturity

Pages: As the children and students of the tarot, the pages are the most immature and naïve within the court. Curious in nature and constantly evolving, the pages lead us toward parts of ourselves that we don't often explore or are just getting to know. These energies introduce us to areas of our experience we might not have previously been open to, but their playfulness and childlike wonder intrigue and delight us as we answer the call and hear their messages.

Knights: The knights are the doers. In tarot they exemplify how, where, and why we should take action and begin the work. They are initiators, learning imperfectly on the job and gaining clarity as they go. They are not afraid to take risks, make mistakes, and evolve as they move. They're typically depicted on horseback to show that forward movement is the way they tackle and react to challenges and conflict.

Queens: The queens are the caregivers of the court. Feminine and soft in energy, they hold wisdom and maturity as they graciously sit upon their thrones. These cards offer insight into the spaces and areas where healing is available. The queens are naturally creative and inspiring as well, often helping us evolve and reimagine our creative process or our intentions for personal growth. They can mark a development of womanhood or the embodiment and evolutions of our sexuality or maternal experiences. These cards teach readers how to channel goddess-like energy and nurture ourselves and others.

Kings: The kings hold authority, and they serve as the leaders of the tarot. Usually exceptional in their chosen fields, they use and direct their skills and knowledge to serve and provide for others. They are an archetype that we can look up to, and they often mirror the areas where we are strong and have claimed authority. They represent notable visionaries or abundant leaders.

All court cards are nonbinary, and all sixteen exist within you.
Remember that every court card is gender fluid and nonbinary. While you'll find gendered language in this book and other tarot texts, there is no gender attached to any of the archetypes. A female-identifying reader is just as much a king as she is a queen, for example. Practice detaching yourself from their external façade and focus more on the energy you feel when in their presence. Consider how you might exude the same energy yourself.

It's also worth noting that all sixteen of the different characters represent one complete personality and person: you. We can't be labeled as just one of these personalities, as we can pull from all their strengths (or display their weaknesses) in various scenarios of our lives. On some days we may dominate in our careers like the King of Wands and quickly transition to a softer archetype like the Queen of Cups the moment we step into our home with our partners. The court cards are just facets of us, and when you're reading them, consider their profiles to be like exaggerated characters in your favorite sitcom, pointing out a specific part of your gifts and flaws, but not showing the completeness of you. Like anything watered down to a system of labels and definitions, from sun signs in astrology to Myers-Briggs personality tests to the Enneagram, we always have discrepancies and exceptions to the rule. Another fun practice when learning them is to ask yourself where this character fits in your life and who they remind you of. Would you consider dating them? Being their best friend? Starting a business together? As you become more familiar with their natures, you'll see mini mirrors reflecting members of your family, long-term friends, and even exes in these cards as well.

Use the court cards as a reminder of who you are and can be, but not an all-encompassing definition of your spirit.

Exercise

Ask your tarot deck to guide your learning and kick-start your journey through the system.

1. Take the cards and separate the deck into three piles:
   - The Major Arcana (twenty-two cards)
   - The Minor Arcana, from Ace to Ten
     in all four suits (forty cards)
   - The court cards (sixteen cards)

2. Pull a card at random from each pile, asking each section the following questions:
   - What Major Arcana lesson
     should I focus on first?
   - What Minor Arcana action
     should I learn about first?
   - What court card personality wants to
     introduce themselves to me first?

3

In Cycles

NUMEROLOGY IN TAROT

The ace through ten in the Minor Arcana represent a cycle, and that cycle follows a story that opens with a clear beginning, takes us through an often tumultuous middle, and closes with a (hopefully) rewarding end. Between the novels we read, the movies we get sentimental about, and the Netflix series we binge, we follow a lot of stories. In fact, we're exposed to so many stories in our everyday lives that we can often foretell what's coming next in a plot, or even develop relationships with the character tropes we often encounter.

These cycles become recognizable—expected, even. That is, until we are asked to look at our own life stories, and then we have no clue what is going on! It's easy to see how others should navigate their peaks and pits, yet when we face twists and turns in our narrative, we tend to run the gamut of emotions and find it difficult to gain perspective. Tarot has a way of shining light on all our unknowns in this very human process, and it can help us take a step back and notice complications as continuations of our stories rather than endings. Although deciphering the cards' messages can be utterly frustrating sometimes, it's a practice that challenges our self-awareness.

I definitely understand why tarot feels foreign and confusing to new readers. We start asking the cards questions about ourselves and realize we have a lot to uncover and understand. I was once an eager reader who would cheerfully flip a card over and end up feeling irritated that a small piece of paper could leave me so stumped. I knew the practice was meant to feel vulnerable and perhaps "mystical" in some ways, but I didn't expect it to feel so overwhelming and detail-oriented too. I vaguely knew there was an elemental association to each suit and that some cards were "darker" than others. I knew and appreciated that every detail of every card was illustrated with intention. But boy, was it a lot to learn and memorize.

Rather than getting lost in the minutiae, I eventually decided to zoom out and learn the cards differently. I stopped trying to learn the specifics of each individual card and started paying attention to the system at large. I reviewed the framework of the deck. I committed to learning the differences between the Major Arcana and Minor Arcana. I identified which area of life each suit represented. I looked at how the parts fit together to complete a whole human experience.

Then I got more specific. I dove deeper into the patterns of the cards so I could start to understand the stories they wanted me to see. I learned numerology and the role of each numbered card in the Minor Arcana. I began to dig back into the details and felt less overwhelmed, knowing that each card represented a specific spot in a storyline.

I can confidently say, after thousands of readings for clients and probably a million (OK, that's a stretch) card pulls for myself, that familiarizing myself with numerology was the most helpful lesson I ever received as a reader. It enhanced my intuitive response to the messages and made my personal tarot practice click. While I'm by no means a numerology expert, I do enjoy sharing this system with new readers and knowing that they'll feel more prepared and armed with another point of reference and "clue" as they navigate each archetype.

What Is Numerology?

Numerology is the study of numbers and their significance. Each number carries a particular vibration and holds information about the trajectory of our lives. They can offer insights on the micro or individual level, helping us consider our relationships with ourselves, or the macro level, offering information about how we might fit into and be influenced by the collective energy of the Universe.

It's a language that breaks down frequencies or "vibes" and structures these energies into a system. Numerology isn't just used in tarot; I've developed comfort and confidence in the numerology of this practice specifically, but I remain fascinated by and curious about the other metaphysical spaces that numerology touches, from astrology to life path numbers, and more.

Learning numerology beats relying on your memory when reading, trust me. Certainly, memorization is one way to learn the fifty-six cards that comprise the Minor Arcana. We can treat them like flashcards, reciting relevant keywords and generalized interpretations until we're blue in the face. Or we can learn to *live our tarot* and immerse ourselves not only in the learning of the tarot system, but in dedication to learning more about ourselves. I promise you the themes and recurring lessons of the Minor Arcana cards will become more familiar. There's a lot of repetition in these cards. Eventually, you'll come to know (and even appreciate!) their nuances.

Remember that we are in the midst of many cycles at once.
Our specific stories can't be consolidated into one tarot card at a time. You, my friend, are way more impactful than you know, and your personal story is too complex to be watered down to a single paradigm.

Perhaps you meet a kind and attractive love interest, but eventually choose to end the relationship because of poor timing or misaligned future goals. They weren't your forever partner, but the next one might be.

You find a job listing that feels unexpectedly perfect for you, so you pack your bags without much planning and move to a new city to take a chance on your growth.

You buy a new home and eventually you outgrow the space, so you move into the next one.

You overcome addiction. You process a loss through grief. You find yourself at the end of a personal healing journey feeling quite different, wiser, and more resilient for when the next challenge arrives.

Many things can happen at the same time. While your career can be prosperous and thriving, showing an "established" point in the cycle, a personal relationship or spiritual healing journey may be just blossoming, making you feel vulnerable and uncomfortable at the same time. As you learn the numerology of the Minor Arcana, hopefully you'll realize you are living and moving through multiple cycles simultaneously.

Nothing is guaranteed, and permanence isn't promised.
When reading the Minor Arcana, remember that nothing is mandatory. If you feel strongly that it's time to jump ship and end a cycle, you can. Your commitment to a new job, hobby, or relationship isn't something that has to last forever. The only "forever" experience is the one your soul agrees to when you come here to be this current living, breathing, moving, human version of yourself right here, right now. You are the creator of your reality, the author of your story, and the divine leader of your life. Most likely, if you feel called to step down from something, you're really just honoring yourself by doing so. Challenge the inner voice that labels any moments of graceful bowing out as "quitting." When reading cards, we not only ask to hear from the most authentic versions of ourselves, we also surrender to an intuitive connection and a voice more loving than our inner critic. It's important to pay attention to and attempt, as much as possible, to silence your self-criticism.

Our assignment is to recognize and repair patterns in our lives so when a door closes, we can improve the quality and enjoyment of each experience when the next one opens. With the tarot, we have a chance to integrate the lessons of previous cycles to make the present more palatable, productive, and passionate. This knowledge of self gives us more power to influence our stories moving forward.

Cycles are not always linear.

While the Minor Arcana and tarot tradition attempt to create a clear path with this numerological system, we can of course stray from it here and there. These cycles are not linear; they do not always have to follow subsequently, one after the other. Instead, we have the dynamic experience of skipping, repeating, and backtracking through certain stages sometimes. Try not to get too hung up on the order of the numbers. Focus on their lessons and know that if you shift backward or skip steps, it's more than OK. The cards' energies are unpredictable, and movement within a cycle is likely an indication that your Spirit Guides have a plan for you.

Aces

Keywords: New beginnings, Fresh perspectives,
Universal gifts, Inspiration, Initial stages

Essence

In order to know when and where to arrive at an event, we usually need an invitation. And with the aces, we are enthusiastically invited into the cycles of the Minor Arcana. In the system of tarot, the ace (1) represents new beginnings, first steps, and present opportunities. They offer us a glimpse of what's possible. Your job upon seeing this number is to decide if this offer excites and intrigues you, and, if it does, to then enthusiastically RSVP "yes."

I consider the four aces to be the purest form of the associated elemental energy (earth, fire, water, and air). They offer a fresh, unbiased start on a path, should the asker wish to take it. Which leads me to an important point I mention to fellow readers and clients about aces that appear in a reading: we do not have to step into this new cycle if we do not want to. Much like we can deny a job offer or a second date, we don't have to see *everything* through.

In the Rider-Waite-Smith deck, these offerings from Spirit are depicted on the card by a floating, disembodied hand extending an elemental gift. This suggests that we haven't integrated or embodied the new energy just yet; we're simply assessing and welcoming its positivity and potential.

When Reading

View these cards positively! Aces are opportunistic and lighthearted, like a breath of fresh air. They offer a chance to reset physically, emotionally, or spiritually. Make sure not to cloud them with self-doubt or feelings of unworthiness. Keep your interpretation of them effortless and at a high vibration. For someone who has been committed to inner work and deep personal healing, these aces and opportunities can feel like the rewards for your labor and dedication to self. The aces are fairly "clean" energetically, so when you're reading them, you can feel assured that you've rounded a corner of the previous cycle and are meeting this new, hopeful energy in divine timing.

Twos

Keywords: Partnerships, Making aligned choices, Establishing balance, Being at a stalemate or crossroads

Essence

The decision is officially made. We've accepted the call of the ace and we find ourselves taking another step forward into the energy of two. The twos in tarot bring about themes of partnership, duality, balance, and choice. We're reaching a more committed stage in the cycle, and we're starting to see the influence of previous responsibilities and others' opinions and perspectives. There's conscious thought and choice in this part of the story and developing balance between these different influences is key.

Take, for example, the Two of Pentacles, which brings about the theme of balancing and reprioritizing time and earthly responsibilities or resources. The Two of Swords indicates a stalemate or imbalance in the mind causing uncomfortable indecision. Life sometimes requires a bit of a juggle. When you're weighing pros and cons, remember that using your best judgment is always key.

When Reading

Consider that there are two parties or perspectives at play here. There is always another factor (a person, place, expectation, etc.) outside of you or who you are reading for. Consider the other side for a more balanced reading.

Threes

Keywords: Community, Sisterhood or brotherhood, Beginning to see progress and recognition for efforts, A potential third party or external energy being considered, Teamwork, Cooperation, Apprenticeship

Essence

Numerologically, three is a communal energy in the tarot. These cards are a humbling reminder that we cannot go through any experience truly alone. While the inspiration, idea, and decision to tackle a goal or begin a journey could have been an individual experience, it will now take some form of external support to truly fulfill it. Teamwork, community, and communication are recurring themes in this part of the cycle.

When Reading

Ask for guidance, accept help, and step outside of your ego. The cards in this phase of the Minor Arcana emphasize community support, strength in numbers, and collaboration over competition. Be mindful of any toxicity or resentment that comes up when you have to let others in, and try to recognize any reliance or unfair weight you may place on receiving validation from friends, colleagues, or peers.

Fours

Keywords: Foundations, Structure, Pause,
Renewal, Inward focus, Stability

Essence

Four is a fundamentally grounding number, and one of my favorite
points of the numerological cycle. Fours offer the opportunity to pause,
rest, and reset through structure and simple (sometimes redundant) routine. While it might seem ironic that we're taking time to pause when
things are really getting going, from an intuitive perspective, it makes
sense that we would take this point in the cycle to catch our breath and
energetically prepare for what could challenge us in the conflict and dis-
ruptions of the fives. It's like our souls are craving a moment to recoup
and reconnect with Spirit, knowing a battle could be around the corner.

This part of the cycle also values sustainability. The initial excitement
and rush of starting and committing to something new have worn off.
By this stage in the experience, your intentions are no longer beginning
to take shape; they're well underway. As the honeymoon phase of this
healing process winds down, consider the long-term sustainability of the
emotional, physical, and mental practices you have been fostering.

When Reading

Know that slowing down is a necessity, not a suggestion. We must pause
and reflect to truly integrate and grow, so stages like the fours are never
a waste of time. Although these cards can feel stagnant, they represent a
much-needed pause to help us bring about the stability and mindset
we need to face the remainder of the cycle and its challenges. You are a
human being, not a machine built to produce and advance constantly.
Reframe and adjust any judgment you might have of these slower periods.

Fives

Keywords: Challenge, Conflict, Loss, Grief, A
need for faith, connection, or spirituality

Essence

Fives symbolize change, for better or worse. If I'm being honest, it's usually disruptive and uncomfortable change. This is the stage in the ace-to-ten cycle where the energy reaches a peak, emotions are explosive, the circumstances are not ideal, and something will have to change to reestablish ease and help us overcome whatever challenge is present. The discomfort and hardship of the fives are what help us learn how resilient and strong we truly are. These obstacles usually redirect our growth in a very authentic way, bringing new perspectives in the face of adversity and improving our characters.

When Reading

First, practice self-compassion and give yourself grace. We all fall sometimes, and beating yourself up for having these troubles isn't going to help you navigate the energy. Become mindful and intentional about how and where you direct your healing energy when the fives come into a reading. Try to find solace in the fact that this is the peak of the experience. It's only up from this temporary low. If you are reading for another, hold sensitive space and be mindful of their difficulties. I suggest you bring a sense of hope and optimism, as you know and trust they can and *will* overcome it, but they must remain aware of the discomfort as they transition through this hardship.

Sixes

Keywords: Advancement, Perseverance, Progress, Regaining a positive outlook, Feeling refreshed, revived, and realigned

Essence

The numerological vibration of six in tarot is welcoming. It settles down the energy from those pesky fives and gives us relief from the turbulent feelings and distracting conflicts we've just endured. Similar to the threes, there are often friends and helpers who appear to guide us in this stage of the cycle, and we can sense that stability is returning again. The beauty of this chapter is that sixes also illuminate a greater connection to ourselves, our purpose, and our reason for the prior difficulty. I call them "I'm a badass" cards. Recall the moments that knocked you down and be proud of the way you dusted yourself off and kept believing you were worthy of more. Know your journey is far from over.

When Reading

When reading these cards, I encourage you to appreciate and integrate the struggles and soul lessons you've tackled. Find some gratitude for the hard times, and express appreciation to anyone in your support system who was there for you along the way.

Sevens

Keywords: Reflection, Contemplation, Assessment, Realignment, Knowledge, Truth, Self-accountability, Discernment, Responsible and committed practices for healing

Essence

Well, it's time to meet another difficult energy in the Minor Arcana. The head we come to in the sevens isn't overtly uncomfortable or destructive, but the energy here challenges our patience and asks us to look inward. The vibration is strange and stagnant with this number. You're likely longing for something richer and more abundant at this point in your experience.

Sevens can confirm that we're ready to reap the rewards of our chosen path and reach the goal we committed to earlier in the cycle. Spirit and the tarot are bringing you another opportunity to engage in self-guided healing, and self-awareness is key during this phase. We can become complacent during this stage if we don't take an honest look in the mirror and assess where we could be more engaged. Rather than numbing out, this number calls us toward another deep dive of inner work, and although waiting for results can be frustrating, it's a necessary aspect of creation and true fulfillment.

When Reading
Look at the facts rather than the feelings. As you read sevens, you may find yourself getting frustrated or impatient with your progress. Triggers could easily arise as this slow-moving energy pinpoints any fears or feelings of unworthiness you might still carry. Audit your life and efforts honestly, make changes where necessary, and resist judging your timeline, your progress thus far, or your character. From my experience as a reader, reading the sevens for another person can either go really well or feel a bit forced. Know that so much of these lessons rely on the person's willingness to integrate or truly sit with the self-awareness required, so try not to take it personally if the message you're channeling or suggesting doesn't feel entirely embraced or received!

Eights

Keywords: Mastery, Craftsmanship, Dedication, Action, Final efforts, Confidence, Self-assurance

Essence
Number eight in the tarot and Minor Arcana cycle is all about progress and culmination as well as what we need to prioritize and give attention to. With all the hard work of the previous numbers, eight indicates that

success is finally at your doorstep—hooray! Energy and excitement are building, and you're well on your way to finishing up this cycle. This number calls for one last push toward mastery. Be ready to show up for yourself and your goals and put more work in to earn the gifts coming soon. The eights tell us that we *can* and we *will*.

When Reading

Commit to the final push. This is the moment to double down on yourself and your healing experience. Whether this part of your journey is asking you to let go of a thought that's holding you back (Eight of Swords), hustle harder toward a goal (Eight of Pentacles), or say goodbye to something that's not serving you (Eight of Cups), these are the last few actions you must take to stay in alignment with your purpose and receive the most rewarding ending to a beautiful story.

Nines

Keywords: Fulfillment, Luck or fate, Reaching a goal, Independence, Harmony, Bliss, Happiness, Exaggerated energy, Overabundance (like the Nine of Swords or Nine of Wands)

Essence

While you might assume ten is the logical ending and completion to a cycle, the finale of the Minor Arcana actually rolls out in two parts. Nine is the apex of the storyline, and this is where abundance (for better or worse, depending on the element) arrives! With this number, the results of the work you've done and efforts you made are apparent and obvious, and you have many lessons that led you here to this chapter that feels like a "payoff."

Nine is a more independent energy compared to the upcoming ten, so notice how/where/if you feel safe within yourself, where you feel prosperous and self-sustaining, and what areas of your life and experience are making you *really* proud right now.

When Reading

Find equal parts pride and gratitude in your journey thus far. While in this fulfilling phase, proudly acknowledge all your hard work and healing. Lean on presence, humility, and appreciation so you can truly embrace this stage and reflect on where the journey has taken you. What's the point of inner work if you don't enjoy the benefits and relief of it? You owe it to yourself to celebrate rather than rush into another cycle.

Tens

Keywords: Cycles ending, Abundance and fulfillment, A time of generosity and giving, Release, Taking responsibility

Essence

Now the true finale arrives! Tens are the last cards in the sequence of the Minor Arcana, and while they bring endings, they also signify a rebirth, a longing for new experiences, and a willingness to dive right back in (through a new ace) for more healing and self-connection. This number is a strong and beautiful reminder that our inner work is never really complete, and it's in our nature to long for more growth and spiritual or personal evolution. We roll our eyes at the challenges that arise and question our abilities to succeed, but the truth is we are built to be resilient, and we enjoy overcoming challenges. The tens in tarot ask us *What's next?* and *What can I share from this experience?*

When Reading

Consider what wisdom you carry that you could share with other people. I firmly believe we are all healers in the sense that our individual paths can inspire, uplift, and unify others who are on similar paths. When you're blessed with the abundance of ten energy in your readings, consider if it's time to take your healing and experiences outside of yourself.

My Full Cycle

While writing this chapter, I realized my tarot journey can be summarized in these ten parts as well.

I stumbled upon a hobby that effortlessly inspired me and intrigued me (ace), then *chose* to purchase a deck for myself (two). I started reading the cards' meanings, asking the internet questions, and considering the perspectives of other readers who had already developed their craft (three). Eventually I found it peaceful, protective, and truly helpful to my personal practice (four). In that phase of my life, I was weathering some difficult storms and turned to my tarot cards in moments of fear and change (five). I found new appreciation for the practice, viewing it as a saving grace and a helpful tool (six). Years passed and my awareness of my psychic gifts strengthened through intentional and repetitive inner work (seven). I worked on my reading skills as much as I worked on myself. I created rituals and committed to constantly showing up for my clients (eight). I eventually found myself surrounded by an abundance of business opportunities and a thriving community based around seventy-eight beautiful cards (nine). I was in awe. I wanted to leave something else to the tarot community, something special and empowering, a book that would support readers when they came to their deck graciously, fearlessly, and completely themselves. And today, you hold that book (ten), so I thank you.

Exercise

Using my example above, reflect on a cycle or segment of your life and write your own ace-to-ten story. Recall the missteps, wins, and lessons you learned along the way.

4

In Practice

RITUALS, ROUTINES, AND PREPARING A READING

We've covered some basics, including best practices, the origin of the cards, and the cycle and purpose of the system they follow. Now we're getting to the good part, my friends. We're going to begin shuffling and working with the deck to see what we are capable of as readers and storytellers. (And believe me: you're capable of quite a bit.) This will be fun!

This chapter could easily become an entire book devoted to rituals, routines, and sacred practices for you to implement in your engagement with the tarot. Instead, I've chosen to offer just the fundamentals for you to explore here. My intention is to share suggestions and ideas and inspire your connection with a new spiritual tool without overwhelming those who are just beginning to dip their toes into tarot as a self-healing practice. In this chapter, I will focus primarily on the experience of reading cards for *yourself*, but everything can be used to provide readings and messages to those you love as well.

Explore . . . Then Establish (and Stick With!) a Routine

My greatest advice as you read and digest these recommendations is to experiment and find what works (and is sustainable) in your practice. I believe it's best to try a variety of approaches for shuffling and pulling cards and preparing yourself before a reading so you can find what feels authentic and allows you to relax and feel truly supported. I always share with my tarot students that reading cards requires a balance of complete trust and surrender. Flow with what feels right while establishing a container of energy that feels grounded, safe, and reliable.

Once you find what "sticks," stick with it! Repetition is important when you begin opening your intuitive gifts because it will help to form a habit of expected actions so that your third eye can have "free rein" and feel supported when opening itself to messages and connections.

Prepare Your Space

When I'm reading cards, it's important that I create a space that's free of distractions, excessive noise, and clutter. Every object in our home holds energy just like living things do, so the more clutter or stuff you have around you during a reading, the more influence there will be on the cards, and the more distracted the messages can become.

Many readers like to designate a specific space in their home for readings, and I think this is a great idea. I tend to pull cards by the altar I've created in my office. An altar is a space that visually inspires and represents our spiritual intention, healing efforts, and metaphysical commitments or learning. It's more than an Instagrammable array of crystals; it's a space that feels sacred to you. An altar can house all the tools you need to practice, including your cards. It can be as large and elaborate as a table full of objects, or it can be as simple as a row of decks and plants on a windowsill. Remember that spirituality does not have to be extravagant. Incorporate this spot into your daily rituals and spiritual work and let it bring you comfort.

What to Include on Your Tarot Altar:

- Your tarot decks, oracle decks, etc.

- Crystals

- Candles or incense

- Photos of past loved ones, yourself as a child, deities you connect with, or any image that feels relevant to your Spirit Guides

- Mementos, notes, or trinkets that feel deeply meaningful and special to you

- Dried or fresh flowers, riverbed rocks, small seashells, or other natural elements

Tip: I also enjoy reading cards outside on my porch or balcony on a quiet morning before the drone of traffic begins to pick up. If you choose to read in nature, notice the supporting elements around you (earth, wind, water, and heat), and appreciate their influence on your reading. You might find you connect more to the suits' elements when you're outdoors.

Prepare Yourself and Your Body

Pulling tarot cards is a form of energy work, and channeling with the cards requires our physical and emotional bodies to exert energy. For that reason, you might notice that your body holds tension in anticipation of you beginning the reading or you may feel exhaustion after reading as a result of the focus and emotions you called upon.

First, I like to shake off any residual stress that may affect my reading with some movement. I'll make sure I work out or go for a walk, or sometimes I'll stand up and literally shake my limbs to invite in a new vibration of alertness and openness. Take some time to center yourself with a few rounds of easy breathing and draw yourself back to your center.

I also sometimes practice a grounding routine to find some peace before I pull cards. These energetic protection rituals are essentially ways to manipulate, move, or expel your energy and settle your frequency so you feel supported in your empathic abilities.

I have a variety of psychic practices and tools I've picked up over the years from teachers and mentors, but I'll walk you through two fundamental and simple steps in my daily protection practice. These can be used right before a reading, when you start your day, or before you interact with other people and their energies or movement.

Grounding Cord Practice

A grounding cord metaphorically attaches your body to the earth, and visualizing this cord via a regular grounding practice can leave you feeling anchored, rooted, and held as you explore and tune into a more psychic dimension. As such, it has become a nonnegotiable in my channeling practice before any reading.

To try it . . .

Sit tall and tune in to your breath. Envision a ball of light attaching to the base of your spine (root chakra) or the bottom of your feet. This becomes your cord of connection.

Once you see and notice the colors and details of this energy, watch it travel like a string from your body, down through the layers of soil beneath you, dropping many miles down until it attaches itself to the very center of Earth. This cord now serves as a pipeline for any energy that feels stagnant, blocked, or dense to flush itself out of your body. I like to visualize my worries and anxieties dripping from my head, shoulders, and belly all the way down the cord for the earth to hold instead of me.

Invite in New Light

Whenever we release and remove energy, we have an opportunity to fill our newfound spaciousness with an energy that is more intentional and helpful. In the second step of my protection ritual, I call in a more supportive vibration. You might find this feels just as refreshing for you as it does for me.

To try it . . .

First, picture a ball of light hovering above the crown of your head. Usually, I visualize this as a white or golden yellow color—bright and cheerful! Picture this orb of light and place your name within it, defining this energy as your own. Ask the light to pull back any energy of yours that you might have recently lost (this could be energy you use to hold space for others). If you have any other additional intentions for this light, speak them and watch the orb grow larger and brighter. Then watch it travel into your body, beginning at the top of your head and moving through the entire channel of your body, filling you with light and pure intention until it reaches the base of your feet. Full of light and healing energy, you have now moved and manipulated your own energy to serve you, and this sovereignty is an empowered and responsible way to proceed with a reading.

You may also feel called to say an extra prayer or intention before reading to keep your energy receptive. An example of such a statement might look like:

> Spirit/Higher Self, please support me
> in this reading by sharing truthful
> messages that uplift, support, and
> encourage my healing journey.

In your journal, practice writing your own opening statement or spiritual intention that could serve you in your readings.

Working with Your Deck

Your deck is your physical tool and greatest ally as an intuitive reader, so prepare to gain a new BFF. The tool itself is an extension of your unique energy and activates your connection as a channel. It mirrors the relationships you have with yourself, your higher self, and your authentic voice. So, your cards should be treated with the same care and awareness that you provide your physical body and mental space. The following practices will aid this partnership by keeping the energy between you clear, defined, and supportive.

Choosing Your Deck

You must be drawn to your deck. It doesn't need to be love at first sight necessarily, but the energy, the art, and the feeling of the cards should naturally draw your attention and pique your interest. I recommend waiting until you find one that feels special to you rather than getting what your friends have or what you've seen featured online.

Use one deck to learn and one deck to heal.

While it's not required to be a reader, you may wish to have multiple tarot decks. I reference the globally popular and most commonly referenced adaptation, the Rider-Waite-Smith deck, in the card descriptions in this book. The Rider-Waite-Smith is my "teaching" deck, which I use to instruct on the cards and their meanings. I learned tarot through this system, and if you're serious about your study, it could be worth getting your own copy of this deck. It is rich in tarot detail but antiquated and patriarchal in tone and imagery. I completely respect and understand if it's not your thing. I've certainly had to compartmentalize my own aversion to its gendered themes and establish balance by collecting more modern decks with card interpretations that speak to me.

I have many well-worn and loved decks that feel much more personal to my energy. These are the tools I turn to when I want to do a reading for myself or a client.

Shuffling

There are truly no right or wrong ways to shuffle. If you (unlike me) are well-versed in fancy card tricks or spent a past life as a blackjack dealer, go for it and show off your skills. I do not have any tricks up my sleeve or *smoothness* to my shuffle. Many readers, including me, hold the deck in one hand and gently guide the shuffle of cards into the other, allowing cards from one hand to intermingle into the other. I've been doing it this way my entire tarot career, and it works like a charm.

Tip: Slow down. My most simple tip for shuffling cards is just slow it down. Don't rush the process of feeling their energy in your hand. Release any pressure to pull quickly and instantly interpret, especially when you're just starting. Be patient with the process.

Use your left hand.
The left side of our body is associated with lunar energy and femininity. Many of us are right-handed, so it might feel like a more uncomfortable side to lead from. It took a lot of practice for me to get used to, but now I hold my deck in my right hand and lead the shuffle with my left. I also pull cards from the deck with my left hand. I recommend trying it and seeing if it works for you. You might notice that the left side of the body feels more sensitive, tuned in, or psychic.

Choosing a Card
Everyone eventually develops their own unique style of handling the cards, but it's comforting to know what other readers do as you start developing rituals. I will cover the two methods of shuffling I rely on most frequently. While there is no right or wrong way to shuffle and pull your cards, these two approaches are great for beginners because they're not overly complicated or intimidating.

1. Fan out and feel.
Shuffle the cards until they feel well integrated and complete. Then fan them out in front of you on a table or the floor. Hover your hand (try the left!) over the cards and slowly feel the energy from right to left. This is a great time to practice tuning in to your physical intuition or bodily sensations when tapping in psychically. Notice sensations in your palm, for example a magnetic pull or a tingling feeling. That's your clairsentience leading you toward the right choice. If a card visually stands out in front of you, choose that one; your clairvoyance (psychic seeing) could

be helping you receive clarity. If you are someone who hears or senses when to stop when you hover your hand over a certain card, you might have great psychic hearing, or clairaudience.

Not only will this fanned-out method help you initiate an intentional and patient card pull, but practicing this way will also help expand your psychic abilities and heighten your sensitivity in receiving more insight with the cards and your intuition.

2. Pull from the top when you're ready.

Another method of choosing a card is shuffling, then pulling one (or multiple) off the top when you feel called. I typically shuffle while thinking about my intention or question (e.g., "What's the energy around XYZ?") and repeating it silently to myself until I feel it is time to take a card off the top of the deck. This is the shuffling ritual I use most often, and because I like to pull many cards in a reading, I find it's much faster than fanning them out!

Fliers

A flier is a card that literally flies or jumps out of the deck as you're shuffling. They can fall to the ground, fall on a table, or turn themselves the opposite way than all the other cards in the deck.

When a flier appears, keep it in your reading. Consider these cards as being supercharged with the intention you've set. They're making their presence known and trying to be seen and recognized. Or it's a sign that Spirit is excited to deliver this urgent message. Fliers are an example of tarot readings coming alive and truly feeling magical because of the synchronicities and coincidences. I'm always surprised by how accurate and necessary the message of a flier usually is. My only rule with these dancing cards is that you recognize the difference between sloppy shuffling and flying cards.

I've noticed that on TikTok and other social media channels, you'll often see readers with five cards flying out every shuffle, which (in my opinion, at least) can feel a bit forced or theatrical. I prefer to wait for one card to truly pop out rather than shuffle in such a way that might lead to more fliers.

Seriously, don't only rely on fliers! Some readers will wait for them, shuffling and shuffling and shuffling until one finally leaps out of the deck. While I appreciate those who have faith that the right card will appear at the right time, I think it's disempowering to always pull cards this way. You'll know in your body and intuition when it's time to cut the deck or pull from the top of it. Trust yourself and your inner knowing.

Clarifying Cards

A clarifying card is an additional card we can pull when the original tarot message isn't providing enough context or clarity. Say you've asked your deck a direct question about your career, but the card you pulled doesn't make much sense at first glance (perhaps it spoke to a theme you typically associate with romance or friendship). If you feel confused, you absolutely have the liberty to ask for more detail and build on this first card by asking for a second or third clarifying card.

Something important to note about clarifying cards is they are not *replacing* the first energy with a "do over." Instead, they are embellishing the original message to make it easier for you to understand. When I need additional information during a reading, I like to restart my shuffle and silently say to myself, the cards, and Spirit that I'm seeking a clarifying card for the original message.

If you feel the urge to pull four, five, six, and so on clarifying cards, I recommend starting the reading over and regrounding yourself. If you have anxious energy taking over, you might benefit from starting fresh with a clearer question or intention, or a more open mind and heart.

Caring for Your Deck

Energetic hygiene is important in all forms of divination, and tarot is no exception! By caring for your tarot deck and making these cleansing rituals common practice, you'll notice more accurate readings, easier connection and communication between the cards, and a more profound healing experience.

You'll know when to cleanse and charge your deck.

I recommend cleansing your deck whenever it feels a bit "off." Don't overthink this—you'll know it's time to recharge when your card pulls don't feel quite as accurate, or you're walking away from a reading feeling less satisfied or inspired than you usually do. But I also recommend taking a few moments to cleanse your deck when . . .

- You purchase a new deck (or someone gifts you one)
- You've performed a reading for someone else using that deck
- You haven't used your deck in a while; it's been resting
- Other people have touched, shuffled, or handled your deck
- You feel like you've been using your deck very often, especially for emotionally heavy readings or difficult questions
- You've traveled with it, attended an event with many people, or have taken it out and about

You don't need to use sacred woods or herbs.

I no longer use white sage or palo santo to cleanse my deck, even though I did for years as a new reader. I made this choice after learning more about the lack of ethical sourcing of these cleansing tools and learning more about them as Indigenous practices. I felt I was dishonoring the tradition and the sacredness of these practices, which is why I chose to develop other cleansing rituals that felt better to me. I've found them to be more respectful and just as effective.

1. Reorder your full deck.

My absolute favorite way to cleanse and reset my tarot deck is to organize them into numerical order, from The Fool to the King of Pentacles. First rearrange the twenty-two cards of the Major Arcana (The Fool to The World), then order the fourteen cards from each Minor Arcana suit beginning with the ace through the ten, followed by the page, knight, queen, and king. I then like to place the cards based on the speed of the element, beginning with earth/Pentacles (the slowest), then water/ Cups, air/Swords, then ending with fire/Wands (the quickest). Finally, I'll place the Major Arcana on top of that, so the top card is The Fool. Once all seventy-eight cards are arranged in order, I allow them to rest for about a day before I use them again.

2. Connect your deck to a grounding cord.

The same grounding cord you attached to your body can be used to release energy from your tarot deck! Place the card deck in front of you, then close your eyes. Visualize the same cord or line of energy attaching to the bottom of the deck and traveling to the core of the earth, creating a line of connection that can be used for release. Take a few deep breaths and visualize any old energy falling away from the cards and down the grounding cord, clearing the deck of previous energies.

3. Use salt.

Salt is an incredibly effective resource for energetic cleansing, and luck- ily, we have an abundance of it in our homes! Using a bowl of whatever kind of salt you have, place your cards on top and allow some salt to slip between the cards or sit on top of them. The deck doesn't need to be entirely covered or buried, just incorporated into the salt. Allow the cards to rest and cleanse for a few hours or overnight. (Due to the potential for salt to attract moisture, I prefer to let my cards rest for a few hours to avoid the risk of them getting water damaged. But you could also wrap your cards in a plastic bag to protect them.) Remove the cards and discard the salt immediately to ditch the energy it removed.

Tip: Salt is an amazing natural purifier. If you're really worried about messing up your deck, cleanse your hands with the salt instead. Rub a bit into your palms while washing them before or after handling your cards or take a salt bath after facilitating readings.

Recharge Your Deck

Recharging a deck is similar to cleansing it, but rather than removing old, stagnant energy, the intention is to infuse it with new energy to enhance the power of the tool. It's especially effective after cleansing your deck first. Just like the energetic preparation of your body and energy field/aura, when we release what's not necessary, we can fill the space with an energy that's more supportive and vibrant.

There are many ways to charge your deck.

1. Let the deck rest.
My number one suggestion is to let your tarot deck "nap." Allow time between your readings, especially if you're noticing your connection or communication doesn't feel strong.

2. Expose your deck to sunlight or moonlight.
Both solar and lunar forces hold beautiful energy that can fill your deck with new life. I prefer to use sunlight, primarily because I use my decks for client readings and professional endeavors, and it infuses it with confident and active solar energy, but a beautiful full moon bath is also incredible for your tarot deck. Simply rest the deck near a windowsill (or outside if your environment allows) during the night of a full moon or on a bright sunny afternoon—your choice! Just note that as you work with your deck more and more, its wear and tear will start to show. Whether they begin to fade from all the sunlight or pick up bent corners from being cleansed and protected, your tarot will age with you as your practice evolves.

3. Use selenite or other crystals.
Many readers like to use crystals like clear quartz or selenite to give energy and life to their tarot decks. I often set my tarot deck on a selenite wand or selenite plate because this particular crystal carries a high vibration that wards off negative energies and simultaneously charges the deck with purity and light.

4. Infuse your deck with sound and healing vibrations.
If you have a singing bowl, you may wish to play it near your cards, as they can pick up on the healing vibration and resonance. Don't have

one? That's OK! You can always stream healing music (typically tuned to certain frequencies) throughout your home, by your altar, or to help recharge your energy after a reading.

Inner Tarot Practices to Develop Ritual and Connection with Your Cards

Introduce yourself to your deck, then ask it to introduce itself to you. This is by far my favorite ritual to move through with a new deck of cards. Whenever I buy or receive a new deck, I introduce myself to it then interview it! Each deck has a different personality, and I firmly believe that decks come into our lives to support us in navigating certain chapters of life with a specific perspective. I have some decks that are very blunt and direct in tone, keeping it real with me when I turn to them for guidance. Other decks are more creatively inspiring and softer in their approach to sharing the messages. I appreciate both!

To introduce yourself to your deck, hold your cards in both hands. Sit for a few breaths in meditation, holding them close to your body so they can pick up on your energy. Quietly state your intention to connect with them and let them know that you understand the work and healing you can do in partnership with this tool. Then begin to shuffle and ask the cards the following "interview" questions:

- What do you appreciate about me and my healing process?
- Where do you want to steer my attention?
- What tone can I expect from you? How will you communicate with me?
- What area of my life are you looking to heal together first?
- What do you feel are my unique gifts and strengths?
- What "weaknesses" could I notice or work on?
- What are you here to teach me?

- How can I best learn from and lean on you as a deck and tool for my inner healing?

Journal for a bit following this practice to soak up the messages and reflect on your deck's answers. Add a date to your journal entry so you can look back and remember the initiation of this relationship and watch how it evolves as you continue working together.

Perform a journaling ritual accompanied by a daily draw.
Learning the cards' meanings and establishing a connection with the cards can take quite a while! It took me years to fully learn and integrate all the themes and meanings, and I always kept my trusty guidebook close by in case I started to draw a blank. But a daily card pull and morning/evening ritual with my deck was a very helpful part of becoming a confident reader.

1. Pull your card.
Through a process and ritual that feels natural to you, pull your card of the day! Get grounded, shuffle, and choose a card using some of the suggestions and practices from this chapter. Draw at random, trusting whatever lesson or theme is meant to come up, or ask the deck something specific.

2. Let your intuition respond first.
In your journal, write your immediate intuitive reactions to the card. Do you feel a certain emotion when you look at it? Are you resistant to it, or maybe relieved? What do you feel this card represents and how are you intuitively picking up on its energy? Take a wild guess about the meaning (you may surprise yourself).

3. Read about the card.
Using Part 2 of this book or other resources, read the meaning and description of the card you pulled.

4. *Make it make sense.*

Using both the card's meaning and your intuitive response (even if they differ), journal, reflect, or meditate on what this card might be trying to tell you as you move through the remainder of your morning or evening routine.

Tarot "Shoulds" and "Shouldn'ts"

I hesitate to label anything in this practice as a "do" or "don't" because we live by so many rules, expectations, and restrictions as it is. Your tarot experience is *yours* to discover, not mine to regulate or try to definitively instruct. But I have made my fair share of mistakes with my tarot readings, and I'm offering these tips in hopes that you develop a stronger relationship with your cards from the start. I've learned what rituals felt odd to me, what practices left me feeling burnt out or overstimulated rather than supported, and today I've finally found what feels sustainable and true to me as a reader.

1. Always remember that you have free will.

Tarot reads the energy of the present moment, but it doesn't tell us exactly what must or will happen; rather, it provides context, information, and perspective to allow us to remain in the driver's seat as conscious beings with control and free will. The cards help illuminate what paths or options could bring us ease. They can also show us the areas where we might find resistance so we can better navigate toward the best possible outcome.

2. Set boundaries for yourself so you don't get obsessive.

Reading cards is fascinating, enticing, and exciting . . . until it teeters on becoming obsessive. If you're "panic pulling" and jumping right into the cards or reaching for your deck any time your anxiety picks up, it could be time to take a bit of a break. Whenever emotions are heightened and our brain is craving another dopamine hit of validation, the tarot can become a crutch rather than a supportive tool. Don't be afraid to set some boundaries between yourself and your deck; try slowing down the frequency of your readings when you're noticing an unhealthy reliance or dependence on them.

3. You're doing fine, so don't overthink it.
The most crippling thing you can do to your intuition is question your immediate feelings and responses. Remain curious about the possibilities but try not to question your capabilities. There's a clear distinction between wondering what more you're capable of tapping into and assuming there's no way you're truly on track with the messages and information you're receiving from the cards.

There is no right or wrong in tarot. *Full stop.* There's absolutely no correct way to foster this practice, and even though it's only human to label our intentions and actions as black or white, release that urge here. When you consciously arrive in front of the cards and connect with yourself and your guides, you're doing everything *just right.*

4. Don't get performative or forceful.
Your tarot readings are yours and yours alone, so don't worry about what other readers are doing or how they conduct their readings. If you see another reader with a different method of pulling or interpreting a card, know that you don't have to question yourself. Intuitive work can bring up a great deal of imposter syndrome and self-doubt, but always keep in mind what makes you feel most comfortable. Forcing yourself and your practice to look a certain way won't feel spiritually fulfilling; it will feel like a new-age version of trying to fit in with the popular crowd.

5

In Support

TAROT SPREADS

Once you establish a connection to the cards, it's almost inevitable that you'll start pulling cards more frequently. At this point, it is likely your curiosity is piquing. The rituals discussed in the last chapter can help you gain familiarity with and consistency in your practice, but this chapter will explore the various ways you can construct a reading and get creative with your tarot card pulls. These spreads can help continue your engagement with the cards and serve as strong spiritual conversation starters.

Why is it so challenging to read our own cards?

Reading for yourself is difficult; this is undeniable. Just like how your therapist shouldn't know you outside of their office walls, you should try to disconnect your personal biases or projections when reading for yourself. (After all, there is nobody closer to you than . . . well, *you*.)

Reading for yourself is the most challenging and rewarding part of your tarot practice, and from my observations, this discomfort seems fairly universal. Many readers, myself included, tend to be pretty accurate when they pull cards for someone else. As a third party, we can objectively view the cards and their messages, observing and holding space for interpretation through an unbiased lens. But as soon as we ask the same questions for ourselves, it's immediately more nuanced and less obvious, and our desires and longing for a particular message to look a certain way can cloud the reading.

Is it impossible to read your own cards? Absolutely not. When a self-guided reading is performed in a grounded way, it can be incredibly powerful and healing to hold that honest conversation between you and you. Just like anything related to our psychic connection and intuitive skills, it just takes practice.

Choosing the right questions to ask your deck can be tricky.
One way to combat the challenge of reading for ourselves is to ask the right questions and set ourselves up for success. Often, we will reach for our tarot deck wide-eyed and excited to see what our intuition can pick up on. We're anticipating an epiphany or psychic breakthrough that will guide our next authentic step or instruct our subsequent movements. Then, we're halted. We realize we have to ask something of the cards, and in searching for a question, we begin to question ourselves, *What is it that I truly need?!*

Tarot works best with a clear ask. And the quality of the question we propose can make or break the reading. The key to asking supportive questions of your deck is to find a balance between empowerment and trust. A reader should feel equal parts confirmation of their inner knowing and surrender to the magic. This delicate balance of control and surrender sets the stage for an immersive and beneficial reading rather than a discouraging one.

After years of missteps in my own readings, I've learned what types of questions leave me feeling calmer and more present and what kind of inquiries cause me to feel dysregulated. I've found that the best questions are open-ended. Tarot is not a Magic 8 Ball, after all. (I know, what a bummer.) Sure, the tarot cards tell the story of a full life cycle, but they aren't outlining your life path like a user's manual. It's your responsibility to take the pressure off yourself and the cards to get it perfect so they can present a helpful reading that's open to interpretation. A reading full of absolutes can feel judgmental, like a scolding from Spirit. In reality, your deck's intention is to share profound lessons that can guide your best judgment and free will.

Below I've listed some examples of disempowering questions and provided more healing replacements:

Instead of . . .

"Will I ever heal?"

Try asking . . .

"How can I continue to support my healing?"

Instead of . . .

"Where is my soulmate? Have I met them before?"

Try asking . . .

"What's a message my vulnerable heart is trying to share with me as I prepare for divine partnership?"

Instead of . . .

"Why isn't my career taking off?"

Try asking . . .

"What's an actionable first step or mindset shift I can prioritize to move closer to my goals?"

Questions for Your Daily Card Pull

In the previous chapter I recommended daily card practices and tips to help you develop an enjoyable routine with your tarot deck. Here are some examples of questions you may want to ask your cards as part of a morning or evening routine:

- How do I encourage myself today?

- What energy might I notice today?

- Are there any lessons I can remind myself of today?

- What is the gift of today?

- Where will I feel and find [passion, connection, truth, help, clarity, etc.] today?

When you begin working with cards frequently, especially through a daily practice, the conversation with your deck is bound to feel a little stale sometimes. When that happens, practice a student's mindset. When I was a new reader and had days when I wasn't particularly inspired by a card's theme (or just didn't find it as relatable or profound to me in the moment), I would do a quick Google search about a new symbol or detail I hadn't noticed before, or write a few affirmations based on the energy of the card to carry with me as I moved on with my morning.

Tip: Remember, energy can't improve drastically overnight, so use your daily ritual as a check-in to inform you of what the day could feel or look like, rather than expecting radical change or instant gratification.

What Is a Tarot Spread?

A tarot spread is a road map for our readings. It outlines the turns to take, like a metaphysical GPS directing us toward our destination and potential clarity. A tarot spread maps out where the cards should be physically placed and arranged after you pull them, as well as what each card in the placement represents through a theme, question, or prompt. I've included many spreads in this chapter for you to explore and dive into.

Tarot spreads are fantastic for new readers because they serve as containers for your reading and allow you to hold clear and definitive space for just a few cards before getting overwhelmed with a more free-flowing reading.

While I don't use tarot spreads in my client readings now, I do turn to them often in my personal practice because they keep me homed in and give me less room to become biased or sloppy and/or to avoid sitting with the cards that I'm not thrilled to see in front of me.

Is it better to use a tarot spread or intuitively pull cards?
Both approaches are powerful! If you're intuitively pulling and asking follow-up questions, you're building a tarot spread as you go. You're essentially allowing the first card to trigger the second follow-up question, building a dialogue between you and the tarot deck.

The best part about tarot is that nothing about the experience has to remain rigid or constant. It's a feminine practice that's meant to flow and support you through adaptability and ease. You can try a tarot spread one day that deeply resonates, then the next day feel called to pull a few more intuitively without boundaries. I recommend experimenting with both and staying patient as you develop your preferred methods and style. The way I pulled cards when I first began reading looks entirely different from what I do today. It's OK to evolve and change!

Create Your Own Tarot Spread
There are plenty of spreads available on social media and in books like this one. Pinterest is actually one of my favorite resources to search for themed tarot spreads. I love creating my own, too! Designing my own tarot spreads feels personalized, like developing a recipe that's perfectly tailored to my needs and taste. If you'd like to try creating your own tarot spread, I recommend fitting the pieces and questions in like a puzzle, following three parts for a well-rounded and helpful self-guided reading.

Take a moment to get really clear on what you're looking to better understand from this reading. What do you want to know or feel after? When you don't set a clear intention, channeled messages often come through jumbled and messy. I recommend writing your question at the top of your journal as a reminder to stay true to that intention before shuffling the cards. This small step anchors your reading and sets the tone for you to succeed.

Part 1: Craft the first question(s) around your internal experience. Make it all about you! You can ask questions about how you're feeling, how a situation is affecting you, or what you feel personally called to change/shift/heal.

Part 2: Next, follow up with a couple questions about the external experience you're facing. Questions about who, what, and which environments are contributing to your energy are all great places to start. This second portion of the spread can help you observe your internal feelings more objectively to better understand how external factors contribute to the emotions and responses in you.

Part 3: This is the meat of the reading, the substance that offers insight into our potential and informs how we can show up for ourselves and in our world after putting the cards away. This part of a tarot spread can explore the *why* and *how* of the information already gathered. I encourage readers to focus on a couple more questions and cards here to emphasize what change or healing is available to them, what could shift energetically, and how exactly to execute the insight and wisdom being offered by the cards.

Inner Tarot Spreads

Two-Card Spreads

(Card 1 / Card 2)

- Problem at hand / A potential solution
- Thought / Action in response
- What is abundant? / What is lacking?

Three-Card Spreads

(Card 1 / Card 2 / Card 3)

- Past influence / Present influence / Future influence
- What to pause / What to start / What to continue
- Your experience / Another person's experience / The energy between the two of you
- Opportunity / Potential challenge / Ideal outcome
- Your current energy / A path to explore / The potential of that path

New Moon Spread

Card 1: Lesson of this last moon cycle to support you in the upcoming phase

Card 2: The energy that is arriving or opening for you through this new moon cycle

Card 3: How you can prepare yourself to receive

Full Moon Spread

Card 1: Inspiration received from this last moon cycle

Card 2: The energy that is leaving or being shed during this closing moon cycle

Card 3: How you can prepare yourself to release

Celebrate Yourself Spread

Card 1: The win

Card 2: The reason for the win

Card 3: What you deserve for your efforts

Card 4: How you can give yourself that reward

Greater Self-Awareness Spread

Card 1: The areas you are choosing to ignore in your healing process

Card 2: Where you make excuses for yourself

Card 3: The actions or influences that take you away from your authentic self

Card 4: How you can support yourself with more kindness

Creative Expression Spread

Card 1: What your energy wants to create right now

Card 2: What your creative energy responds well to

Card 3: What your authentic self wants to share with the world through creativity

Card 4: A clue or hint about accessing your creativity

Card 5: Spaces for creativity and expression that are yet unseen or unnoticed

Intuitive Development Spread

Card 1: Your intuitive connection today

Card 2: The energy that's available to you and your intuitive process

Card 3: What to try differently when connecting with your intuition and Spirit Guides

Card 4: A message from Spirit

Card 5: A feeling or energy you can access when you're living outwardly rather than focusing on your inner connection

Divine Love Spread

Card 1: The love you want to give

Card 2: The love you hope to receive

Card 3: The energy of your self-love

Card 4: The energy of your love with others/someone else

Card 5: The healing potential that is available in your relationships/heart

Card 6: How to communicate those needs and healing in your loving relationships

New Year/Chapter Spread

Card 1: The challenge of this last year/chapter of life

Card 2: The gift or lesson of this last year/chapter

Card 3: What you learned about yourself or how you changed during the year/chapter

Card 4: The intention to hold for the upcoming year/chapter

Card 5: An energy to be aware of this upcoming year/chapter

Tip: You can then pull one card per month for the upcoming season, chapter, or year. Beginning in the month you are in currently, forecast the energy ebbs and flows with a "year ahead" spread. This can be any number of months. I typically choose between three months, six months, and a full year.

6

In Shadow

READING REVERSALS

All seventy-eight cards and archetypes are powerful and profound, but, like everything else, they have polarities that swing between shadow and light. We could label these aspects as cons or flaws, but, just like us, the tarot is imperfect in some ways. When a card stares at us upside down, we are forced to flip our own perspective to look at it with a new one. A reversed card can signify that its theme has taken on a darker, denser, or more complicated energy. By learning to read reversals intuitively, we have an opportunity to not only bring more diversity and variety to our readings, but also become more comfortable and honest about the complexities and hardships of our human experience.

What Is a Reversal?
To put it plainly, a reversed, or flipped, card is one that faces the opposite direction than the other cards in a reading. Most often, it will be upside down while the others are right side up. The tarot community often speaks of these cards with mysticism or concern, and when I

first started teaching others the basics of tarot, I got questions about reversals *all the time*.

The moment students discovered that reversal cards were a *thing* from the guidebooks that came with their decks, they felt scammed. They were now being asked to learn and memorize the nuanced meanings of not one but *two* versions of each card! I completely understand the overwhelm and aversion to reading them. A tarot deck has a plethora of detail, even before this second layer of complication.

But as intimidating as they might feel in the beginning, readers will quickly realize that reversals bring a more accurate and instinctive understanding to our channeled messages. The key is finding your own comfort level with them, defining the time and place you prefer to read them, and using a looser, more intuitive style of reading when working with the Tarot.

A flipped card shows us that its energy is generally lower, less potent, or harder to see or define in the moment. These shadows are meant to make us pause and think (since our vision of the card is immediately blurrier), then address our lack of clarity and go further in our intuitive investigation.

When we are pulling an abundance of cards in the reversed position, it could mean that we are consulting tarot from a place of fear rather than faith, and we're generally questioning ourselves in our lives or in our readings.

Why do reversals show up in readings?

Simple! For the same reason our clothes can be put away inside out or our socks can get placed in the underwear drawer: because we're messy and we miss the details sometimes. The most logical reason is that the card got flipped around and out of order as we were shuffling or when we were putting them back together at the end of the last reading.

However, there are readers who are meticulous about reordering and putting their deck away without any reversals at the end of a reading, yet still the occasional card will end up out of alignment, and that's where the magic of tarot can be felt.

These upside-down energies are the perfect example of how our decks are "living" objects that carry our personal and sacred energy, so it's no coincidence that they have their flaws, quirks, and imperfections just like we do.

Do I have to read reversals?

Second only to "What is a reversal?" the other question I'm most frequently asked is if we need to read the card in shadow at all. New readers often wonder about this, which is understandable because reversals are confusing. And before I continue with the explanation, I'll give you the short answer: *No*, you do not have to read them. (Insert a sigh of relief, right?)

The reason you don't have to read them is because you don't have to do anything that feels inauthentic in your tarot or healing process. Reading tarot should never feel pressured or performative. If the idea of reading reversals seems daunting to you, I suggest you get comfortable with the cards in their upright position first so you can better understand and identify their shadows when you do start to read reversals. Having a basic understanding of a card's natural tendencies or "pros" makes identifying its "cons" and red flags much easier. This does not mean you have to know each upright meaning like the back of your hand, but their meanings shouldn't feel like strangers, either.

If you don't want to read reversals for whatever reason, I recommend that you clarify this preference with yourself (and with Spirit and your tarot deck) before shuffling. You can do this by stating to yourself, either silently or out loud, that "all cards will be read as their intended upright meanings," no matter the position they show up in your reading.

To this day I often make this distinction with my own tarot deck, especially if I'm noticing I'm having trouble connecting with it or if I'm anxious about the topic I'm inquiring about. If I feel I'm not in a space to decipher "mixed messages" and would rather keep the reading straightforward so I can truly integrate the message (rather than make excuses), I clarify with my deck that I'm not reading reversals, and I ask for all meanings to come up in their intended upright position.

Speak your needs during your practice, and the beautiful part to witness is how the cards respond and respect your personal boundaries.

What makes reversals so difficult to decipher?

Reversals are frustrating because they represent blocked, stuck, or weaker energy, making their messages less obvious. They are literally highlighting what we can't see, so no wonder we feel blind! They make us hesitate because we intuitively sense something is a little bit *off* with the shadow energy, yet sometimes we can't quite pinpoint what it is until we dive deeper into the reading and our inner knowing.

You will not find precise or exact reversal definitions in this book because my relationship with reversal cards has shifted throughout my years of practice. I've learned to embrace a more intuitive, less prescriptive approach to comprehend them. However, because they share common themes, I've been able to access new ways of understanding them, which I've listed here.

How to Intuitively Read Reversal Cards

A direct opposite meaning

A traditional way of reading reversals is to apply the direct opposite meaning. This isn't my favorite approach. Consider reading this way if you flip a card over that feels very contradictory to what you're experiencing (such as The Lovers when you're newly single). I've noticed across my years of reading tarot that if a card is meant to be read in reversal, it will intuitively hit you like a ton of bricks. You'll sense that the message is meant to take a 180. However, I've found that this isn't common. I don't recommend relying on this method of reading for two reasons.

First, it requires that you know the full deck and all the card meanings upright in order to apply the opposite meanings to each. This feels arduous to me and like a game of stiff memorization rather than organic integration of the patterns found in the cards.

The second reason is that there are likely other cards that could have shown up upright in your reading to offer a similar message as the reversed card. For example, with this approach, the Ten of Pentacles reversed could be interpreted as shallowness and a sense of lack and destabilization, much like the Five of Pentacles. While this way of reading reversals is quite commonplace in tarot, I also feel the deck is so varied and the system covers so many themes. If there was a card that perfectly fit the meaning and intended message already, wouldn't it have shown up instead of resorting to the need for a reversed interpretation?

So, if you're new to reading, this can be a wonderful place to begin your tarot reversals, but I challenge you to reference and consider the other examples below for a more nuanced message.

A spiritual and/or emotional blockage
Reversed cards sometimes indicate energetic blocks or spiritual suspicions. When our limiting beliefs or shame override our true essence, we are left questioning more than is necessary. A reversed card in this instance could represent what we feel unsure about, unworthy of, or emotionally unprepared for. Our resistance is valid, but it can disrupt the flow of energy between us and the Universe and disempower our healing process. Take, for example, the Nine of Cups. Upright, it's a card of deep gratitude, joyfulness, and presence. If someone feels unworthy of those sensations or is unfamiliar with what it feels like to exhale and relax into such a blissful state, they could energetically push it away or limit their capacity to receive it. Subconsciously (or consciously) we can believe certain gifts will never be our reality, and in this example the reversed position of the card shows us what healing is available if we were to work through it with intention. We can challenge the card's position, begin to get to the root of what truly "blocks" us, and align ourselves with what we deserve by incorporating conscious efforts, practices, and self-reflection to remove and release the stagnant experience. We can interpret the reversed message as a catalyst to push us to take our healing into our own hands.

A physical delay
My *favorite* (that's sarcasm) scenario is when a card implies that "This is coming to you! Promise! Just . . . not yet," or "You're almost there, but

we have a few more lessons and detours before you arrive." Welp, it's not ideal if the reversed energy is representing a physical delay or stall in the timeline, but it is a beautiful opportunity to rest in the belief that there is divine timing at play and universal protection surrounding you. If what you want to manifest is taking its sweet time, try to loosen your grip on expectations and allow the energy to flow more effortlessly or focus your attention elsewhere for some space.

An internal experience rather than an external experience

Mostly relevant in the Minor Arcana, this is when a reversed energy is guiding you inward. The Minor Arcana represents our physical experience and external factors, such as our relationships, environments, and more. But what if the card was appearing reversed to take you out of that experience and guide you back inward? The Two of Cups reversed could be read negatively, like your relationships are misaligned or unbalanced. But you could also see it as the card guiding you toward truer self-love, asking you to be your own partner and mirror love and unity back to yourself rather than looking for it in others. The Five of Swords represents conflict and malice between parties in its upfront form, but what if nobody is truly in conflict with you and instead the reversal is relating to a habit of self-sabotage or mistrust between *you* and *you*.

An inauthentic/unhealthy version of that energy

This example is quite common when the court cards show up reversed. They tend to highlight an aspect of their personalities that is unhealthy, egotistical, or inauthentic. When we are becoming hyperfocused on just one aspect of our gifts or strengths, the reversed card could be illuminating where we could soften or "tone it down" in how we show up and show off our personal power. There are many examples of this in the Major Arcana as well. When the Emperor is reversed, it can represent controlling behavior or even toxic masculinity. The Lovers reversed could represent some deep-seated codependences. The reversed Hierophant could depict an unhealthy representation of spirituality, perhaps an experience where faith and religion feel oppressive rather than supportive.

Overabundance or defining yourself by an energy

Another option is that the deck is showing you an area of your life that you're putting too much emphasis on or giving too much focus. It can mean you are beginning to define or limit your potential, expressions, or experiences. An example is the Ten of Cups reversed, which could represent someone who is fixated on home life, children, and family, perhaps even defining themselves by their family unit rather than creating true balance across other independent areas of their life. This reliance can come through as a shadow, highlighting a space for further healing.

Avoidance of that energy

Opposite to that, I've seen reversals come out that poke and prod at a feeling or theme that we do *not* want to address or look at within ourselves. Sometimes when I'm reading for a client, I'll see reversals as a hint of what they are avoiding or sweeping under the rug. It could be an emotion or a part of their personality they aren't proud to express or share, but either way, as a tarot reader I know to proceed with caution and compassion. A great example of this would be the Five of Cups, which is a card of worry, sadness, and grief—emotions many of us want to run away from if we can. The reversed position could be sharing that they are being emotionally avoidant, closing off their hearts, and refusing to be vulnerable and *fully* feel it.

Energy of the past influencing the present

Say you pull something like the destructive Tower or the painful Three of Swords, but, thankfully, those themes aren't relevant in your life right now. In these instances, sometimes a reversed card can reference memories or instances from the past or parts of our stories that are no longer prominent but still impact our experience and views. Those difficult memories or old wounds build our resilience and become our points of reference when we tackle new challenges and rely on our strengths. If you pull a reverse card that feels "old" in energy and relevance, consider how these themes impact and steer your healing today.

A true wildcard/an option you never considered

Wildcards are a pleasure to read and deliver. While this book is meant to guide a personal tarot practice first and foremost, it's almost inevitable that you'll start pulling cards for close friends and loved ones when you connect with your tarot deck. And if you pull something reversed for someone in your life, you could be shedding light on a path they never thought to follow. Maybe you can steer the reflection and conversation with "Have you ever thought of . . . ?" and show them what they were once blind to.

Exercise: Reversals in Your Personal Practice

First, set a clear intention with your tarot deck by shuffling and letting the cards and your Spirit Guides know that you are exploring unseen or uncomfortable energy for this reading. Complete your physical ritual, shuffling and preparing the cards as you see fit.

Read the following four cards in the reversed position. Intentionally read them as a "reversal" to practice and become more accustomed to their shadows. Pull using the following tarot spread, and reflect on each prompt:

- **Card 1:** What's currently blocked in my personal healing? Are there any mindsets, behaviors, or perspectives I'm not considering?

- **Card 2:** What energy am I not noticing in my life right now? What resource or energy is available to me that I'm missing?

- **Card 3:** Are there any opportunities or untapped ideas I should consider that I haven't before?

- **Card 4:** What is a "shadow" I should be mindful of? What flaws, imperfections, or characteristics could I bring more attention to?

Part 2

7

In My Body

THE SUIT OF PENTACLES

The Suit of Pentacles, associated with the earth element, asks us to *get embodied.*

Our soul rests within a human container—a body—and that body quite literally carries us through every single emotion we experience, every pattern we create, and every choice we encounter. It's a physical memory bank for our spiritual experience.

The Pentacles, or Coins, suit governs the physical realm and relates to our physical health, home, abundance, money, security, and safety. Every time I teach this part of the deck, I say the same thing to kick off this elemental journey: "If you can see it, smell it, touch it, or hold it, it's represented in the Pentacles suit." This is a rule of thumb that all tarot readers can look to when they encounter the Pentacles. There is a quantifiability with these cards. We can count on them just like we can count on our bodies for information about what we need to feel safe and secure.

As a psychic and professional intuitive, some might be surprised how much I emphasize the body and talk about grounding and protecting the physical vessel. The first reason I do this is because I recognize that our bodies are incredible, and I am always in awe of how they receive and store intuitive information. Our physical senses speak to us just like our psychic senses; they're keenly aware. What this means is that our bodies sometimes know more than our conscious minds, similar to how our psychic senses can process (and store) the most subtle information. The second reason is that our body holds our story. Some of my clients have given birth or have healed after miscarriages, and others have over-come terminal illness. Some have battled physical addictions, and many of them, like me, have overcome disordered eating patterns that weren't serving them. No matter where our stories and memories match or differ from one another, the common denominator is that all of us have a body that carries us through this life on Earth.

Years ago, I would roll out the yoga mat I purchased from Target in my bedroom. It was the kind of thin and cheap (and often slippery) mat that gets crinkles in it if you leave it folded or rolled up too long. I would turn on beginner YouTube videos, and I'd flow through yoga postures and sequences each evening in an asana practice. I would blast music, and the more I practiced, the more I noticed my breath added a rhythm to my practice, too. My movements were usually awkward, and my alignment was poor, but my effort was honest. I couldn't afford classes at that point in my life, but I looked forward to using the time to decompress and make shapes with my body that I never had before. I'd practice in front of a mirror in my underwear and watch myself, blown away by the movement I was capable of. Sometimes after the YouTube class would end, I'd keep flowing, syncing my breath to my movement for just a bit longer, exploring my body from the safety of that chintzy yoga mat.

I was four years into recovery for my eating disorder at that point, something I had worked on in an intensive outpatient program, or IOP, for multiple months when I was just nineteen years old (for those unfa-miliar, it's like rehab). It was during that stint in treatment that I spoke up about my sexual abuse for the first time, and my therapist suggested a higher level of care and more specialized PTSD therapy, to which I said, "Absolutely not." With defiance, I told my incredibly supportive (yet helpless) parents that I was *done* with doing the hard healing work, and I checked myself out of the program and considered myself healed.

Spoiler alert: I most definitely was not.

At twenty-three, I found myself back in an IOP, reluctant but ready. This time, I was focusing not on my eating disorder, but on the trauma that still lived in the bones and cells of my body. I would return home from long days in group and individual therapy sessions with a binder of printouts with notes and doodles across them tucked under my arm. I remember feeling like such a loser during this chapter of my life. I was so young but cripplingly anxious, beautiful yet unable to see how. I was privileged enough to be able to receive specialized support (but so bitter that I needed it). But each night I would get on my yoga mat, and then for whatever reason, the inner critic would start to silence. I'd enjoy myself, getting lost in the somatics.

No longer punishing or starving myself through an eating disorder, my body and I were progressing. But I still felt like I was in limbo, living between free and "recovered" and not quite. I wanted to come home to my body once and for all, and I had this intuitive feeling that yoga could be the modality to bring me back.

I remember the homecoming. I was facing my mirror in a High Lunge (Utthita Ashwa Sanchalanasana). My left leg stepped forward, and my arms were raised high when I felt *something* shift. I felt my body take the biggest exhale, and I began sobbing. I felt energetic roots grow through my legs, and the strength of my body took over, anchoring me in a space that had always been mine—my body, my home. I had never exercised with an intention of self-love before. I had never challenged myself physically for the sake of growth. I was so used to shrinking my body and hiding it, and that was the first time in a long time (maybe ever) that I was able to feel at peace physically. Today I understand why my body reacted so viscerally, with tears: it felt safe enough to release the pain I was storing inside of it. I could have never known that yoga postures would be like a code that unlocked many new doors, keys that let me finally open myself to the abundance and wholeness that were available to me all along.

Captivated by whatever it was I had just tapped into, my yoga practice continued from there, eventually leading me to a work-trade at a local Ashtanga studio for a while. Then I took part in a yoga teacher training. I later came up with my own style of intuitive movement classes to share with others. To this day, I incorporate somatic movement in my healing work and group workshops. The mind-body-spirit connection is something I believe in deeply. The more in touch we are with our physical bodies, the more we're capable of channeling and receiving intuitive messages from Spirit.

When I began reading tarot cards, I brought a similar mentality and commitment as I did with my asana practice. Reading cards is a physical ritual as well. As you shuffle and move the pieces of paper, the cards flutter and dance in your palms, creating a flow of their own. The more mindful and still you become, the more their messages can move you.

My advice for all readers is to keep showing up to your tarot deck and keep bringing an honest effort and intention. The Pentacles suit is no stranger to hard work, which you'll notice as we navigate this earthly experience and cycle in these cards. Tarot, just like our yoga flows, is most supportive when we practice repeatedly, often enough to build muscle memory.

Just like a beginner yogi learning the poses, your card pulls may feel awkward at first. Give them time to integrate and sink in. There will be a day, similar to my moment in that strong and steady lunge, where a sweeping exhale will move through you as you look down at the cards you've pulled and feel a full-body confirmation. You'll be impressed with yourself. You'll be in awe of what your intuitive body can lead you to. That moment of complete trust in your intuition is a direct result of your commitment to show up and repeat the rituals, routines, and actions that support your inner healing and personal transformation. Once your body feels secure and safe, you will be ushered into new areas of your psychic experience and intuitive gifts.

If you're anything like me, you might fall in love with what your body is capable of and how your intuition moves through it and speaks to you through physical cues. Once your body feels grounded and familiar with what a channeled experience or intuitive message feels like, you can be guided toward new areas of your psychic connection, and your gifts can emerge.

Before we get too ahead of ourselves, let's take some time to move like the earth element and the richness of the Pentacles suit: slow and steady.

Suit of Pentacles Associations

Element: Earth

Chakra: Root

Timing and speed: One season (three months) to multiple years

Astrological signs: Taurus, Virgo, Capricorn

Season: Winter

The Suit of Pentacles is . . .

Grounding, Abundant, Resourceful, Loyal, Familiar, Traditional, Physical, Connected to the material world

When Reading for Yourself

Direct your efforts. Use the Pentacles cards to direct your investments. This could include your monetary investments, sure, but it could also point to the currencies of your time, attention, and skills. The cards in this suit can show you what's going well, what's not, and if you're working hard enough to achieve the results you long for. Think of these cards like a performance review from a manager or boss, but with more *magic*, of course. Be sure to respond to them with action! When you pull them, consider ways you can implement and embrace the Pentacles energy through some physical ritual. Let their lessons guide you toward productivity and remind you to get off your booty, move your feet, and use your hands to make things happen. Then watch the rewards roll in.

When Reading for Someone Else

The tradition of tarot dates back far longer than us baby witches have been sharing tarot cards across our Instagram stories. I encourage you to find the balance between an intuitive response to a card and the traditional messages of the tarot. This blend has always served me well, and I am confident this is where you'll tap in to your best and most confident embodiment of a reader and space holder as well. Call me old-fashioned, but getting good at something takes time. Earning trust from another person takes time. There's no lack of time and patience in this suit, so settle in. The rituals you practice, the commitment and deep respect you hold for each individual card (in the Pentacles suit and outside of it), as well as the unconditional respect and loyalty to those you read for, will determine how seamless and comfortable your tarot experience can feel.

The Pentacles is a suit of integrity, and over my ten years of reading personally and professionally, I've most admired the readers who bring this tradition to their readings rather than utilize fearmongering tactics or outlandish predictive techniques. This is how tarot is often portrayed in movies and sitcoms, and it feels anything *but* authentic. There are numerous examples of how tarot has been bastardized in movies and media, pop culture, and social media virality. It's not a party trick or silly card game. (I know if you're reading this book, you've probably already realized this, but it's always worth reiterating.) Make the experience of learning cards sacred. Take your time, find a grounded and realistic tarot relationship, and enjoy the practice and depth of the lessons for a lifetime.

Tip: Notice any examples of stubbornness in yourself and those you read for. Grounded and practical, Earth energy is stubborn and unwilling to budge sometimes. You may see in Pentacle-laden readings that there's a little less emotion, a lot less passion, and less character and charisma than a reading that has a balance of all four suits. It might even feel like a Pentacles-heavy reading is missing some pizzazz and fun. Being risk-averse isn't wrong, but our experience and healing aren't meant to feel mundane. If the energy feels this way and you (or the soul you're reading for) feel "stuck" at all, ask the deck what to do to shake it up and get out of this rigidity or stale energy.

Tarot Outside of the Deck

In life and in your tarot practice, find what makes you feel safe. Many of us seek thrills, and there's nothing wrong with that! But once you've found the right people and environments that offer you supreme safety, forgive yourself for the times you didn't prioritize your peace and instead found yourself in spaces or places that didn't serve you. Forgive yourself for the moments you chose something or someone that disrupted your foundation instead of working with you to build the life you deserve. The same goes for any faith-based or spiritual practices. When something feels like home, allow it to become a tool, practice, or resource for your soul to reside.

Exercise

Focus on your worth. Consider how good you feel about yourself and how worthy you feel when receiving gifts, money, time, compliments, or *anything* from others. The earth element wants you to ask for *more* from yourself and the Universe. I'm not talking about spiritual bypassing (i.e., "You can manifest your way out of your current reality overnight!"). The Pentacles exude a quiet worthiness that is deeply rooted and committed. It's not showy, but certainly engrained. The Pentacles serve as your permission to draw in (and work for) more until you gain everything and anything your authentic self deserves. You are so worthy.

In My Body | Ace of Pentacles

I shuffle and feel the gentle flutter of tarot
*   cards against my palms.*
They begin to dance.
My left hand guides the choreography.
On this dance floor, I feel at home.

Keywords: Manifestation, Potential, Growth, A path toward security, The beginning stages of a prosperous new venture, A space to land and new ground to build on, A relationship, opportunity, or experience that promises abundance

Meaning

The Ace of Pentacles feels the most literal of all the aces to me; its gift is typically something we can measure. Extending a hand with a gracious offer, Spirit is giving us something tangible and opportunistic to grab ahold of. Consider this an invitation to invest your time. Don't second guess your hopefulness because there's great potential here. It's a card that shows the stable beginnings of something that could grow and withstand the test of time. It could be time to plant roots in a new city or house, begin taking steps toward a career that feels more aligned, settle into the next stage of a committed relationship, or welcome a new addition to your family. The earth element nurtures you as you plant seeds for new energies to bloom.

Be gracious. Stay appreciative and ready. You are inviting miracles in physical form.

Connect to the Ace of Pentacles

Place your body in the hands of Mother Earth. One of the most accessible, simple, and truly effective forms of grounding is to find a patch of grass or soil and plant yourself there. Take the deepest breath of your day and visualize the earth element making its way into your physical body.

I often close my eyes and envision the earth's energy growing through the roots of my feet, up my legs, and through my entire body until I'm standing taller, prouder, and stronger.

Deeper Reflection
Make a vision board. Does it have to be a magazine clipping collage littered across a poster board? No, though it certainly could be! Your vision board could look like a journal entry mimicking your future memoir, a Pinterest board with curated sections, or a drawing you sketch freehand. Your choice. This ace wants to give us something, so show the Universe what's on your wish list! Get as specific as you need to. Create the reality you are willing to work toward.

In My Body | Two of Pentacles

The roots of expectation and assumed
responsibility fall away from my feet,
Leaving me ungrounded, unsure.
The empowered ability to choose sinks in;
I can go anywhere I feel called to be.

Keywords: Adaptability, Flexibility, Balance, Resourcefulness, Patience, Decisions, Open to change, Reallocation of time, energy, and expenses

Meaning
The Two of Pentacles throws a couple different energies our way, then asks us to learn how to juggle. This card is about maintaining balance while caring for and nurturing multiple priorities at once. Time is precious, and the Two of Pentacles reminds us how important it is to notice where and how that time, attention, and energy are being spent.

Because the card here is a two, there is a looming choice or decision on the horizon, but it really isn't urgent. If anything, it would serve you best to continue this juggle and remain even-keeled and responsible with your earthly endeavors. I use the example of an aspiring entrepreneur balancing their "side hustle" with their full-time job to carry their family's (and their own) needs. Create a budget, set a schedule, and remain calm as you continue to navigate your many responsibilities.

Connect to the Two of Pentacles

Practice the art of saying maybe and getting comfortable with it. The Two of Pentacles wavers between black and white and feels most comfortable in gray space. Perhaps we can give ourselves a bit more grace when this card comes around. Would it be the worst thing to say maybe rather than commit to something you're not sure about? Would it be terrible to respond with "I'm not really sure" rather than faking a firm answer to appease someone else? Perhaps it's in the surrender of not knowing that we can remain the most trusting of ourselves.

Deeper Reflection

In your journal, write a list or respond freely to the following prompts:

- I'm still deciding on . . .
- I'm still unsure about . . .
- It's OK to keep exploring before committing to . . .

In My Body | Three of Pentacles

"I could use your help"
used to feel as vulnerable as professing my love,
admitting defeat, or saying I'm sorry.

Healing required me to ask for the support
I didn't believe I deserved.
The friends, the lovers, the family kept showing
*   up for me*
as I kept breaking down to rebuild.

Keywords: Teamwork, Collaboration, Collecting knowledge, Progressing toward work and goals, Utilizing resources, Seeking support and knowledge of others, Studying, Self-betterment

Meaning

We are constantly learning and experiencing new things, even unintentionally. Sometimes we absorb new information simply through observation. The Three of Pentacles asks us to put forth a more conscious effort to improve, act on, and utilize others' perspectives to enhance our own. This card is also a humbling reminder that we don't know everything. We must lean on the skills and expertise of others to tap into and develop our talents. We can be inspired by others walking on their paths toward mastery and purpose and use their successes and pitfalls as knowledge of our own.

The Three of Pentacles presents a fantastic test of both collaboration and self-awareness. The divinity of the triangle as a symbol of stable structures and great foundations represents an underlying theme here. As a collective, we grow, prosper, and evolve through community and connection. If this card is showing up in a professional reading, the statement is clear: work as a team and watch the energy of your work increase exponentially. No matter the intention of the reading, notice the team you've built around you, welcome in more expansive and helpful resources and allies, or consider what expert and trusted voice you'd like to learn from next.

Connect to the Three of Pentacles

Outsource. Ask your mother-in-law to help with the kids one afternoon, call your best friend for a spur-of-the-moment favor, or hire the ideal person for a job you've been putting off. It could be time to ask for additional hands as you juggle the many tasks and requirements asked of you. If you're a business owner, this could mean hiring a new social media coordinator or bookkeeper. For a new parent, this could be ordering grocery delivery because you just *can't* today. Trust that no matter what it is that you need, you're worthy of receiving it, so go ahead and make the call.

Deeper Reflection

Write and reflect:

- How comfortable am I admitting that I don't know everything?

- How often do I seek new knowledge?

- What part of me resists being imperfect, wrong, or not self-sufficient?

- How is my independence helping or hindering my growth?

Answer these questions in whatever context makes most sense to you. You can emphasize your professional life, romantic relationships, or friendships.

In My Body | Four of Pentacles

Hungry for a life that fulfills me,
I'm learning the difference between satiated
and satisfied.

Keywords: Guarding, Hoarding,
Conserving your resources, Control,
Having just enough, Security and
stability without abundance or wealth,
Frugality, Mindfulness of material gains

Meaning

The Four of Pentacles answers the common question "How are you?"
with "I'm getting by."

Just *getting by*?! While the fours in tarot offer us a chance to take a
breath and pause, the stubborn earth element will stop you right here in
the cycle, sit you down, and warn you to stay put. This card resists the
unknown, and the fear of losing what has been established could start to
outweigh our longing for more. While this energy is traditionally about
saving money, the concept of saving or hoarding oneself can span across
many areas of life.

The imagery in the Rider-Waite-Smith shows a man with a golden
coin nestled under each foot as he clutches another, keeping all his
riches (which aren't anything impressive, by the way) close to his chest.
The question to ask yourself is what exactly are you guarding or with-
holding? Is the card showing up in a reading to point out a message
about your wallet, or is it bringing attention to the walls around your
heart? That's for you, the reader, to decide, but know that your life has
the capacity for *more* if you loosen the grip.

Connect to the Four of Pentacles

Address your money wounds. We all have them. Raise your hand if you had to grapple with some deep-seated money fears in your twenties and thirties (here I am raising mine). Our relationship with our finances is usually entangled with our family. Money holds memories—trauma for some, purpose and attachment for others. Money is loaded with so many different connotations. Our parents had their own relationships with money long before we knew how to count those coins from our piggy banks. And their parents learned and passed down their own money stories to them.

Try to recall your first money memory. Ask your family members about their experience with money, too. I also associate this card with a fear of being seen and vulnerable. Sharing any money woes you might have, or hearing others' concerns, can help you begin to mend the money insecurities, abundance blocks, and financial fickleness that might have been present for generations.

Deeper Reflection

In your journal, reflect on the following:

- Do I trust myself to uphold my values (and maintain my valuables)?

- In what ways does my treatment of materials and stuff reflect how I treat myself?

In My Body | Five of Pentacles

It's strange to realize
that every part of me that was once broken
was somehow still
strong enough
to build the life I longed for.

Keywords: Lack, Depletion, Deep worry, Unstable environments, Poor health, Isolation

Meaning

I know the moment this card is flipped over that I'm running on empty. My body is tired and depleted, and I'm tired of feeling this tired.

This card can feel low, a bit hopeless, and lacking. It depicts a frigid winter and two less-than-able-bodied people wandering through its cold darkness. It can mark a chapter of loss, natural disaster, or feeling left out in the cold by family or society. It illustrates a feeling of being forgotten rather than nourished. It's bleak in tone, but the Pentacles cycle is now reaching some kind of peak. The only way out is *through* the Five of Pentacles. The body feels empty in some sense, but the ability to refill and refuel is also here, tempting us to find the strength and resilience to overcome rather than give up. The Five of Pentacles card isn't here to mock your lows but rather validate your hardships while encouraging hope. Since the Pentacles suit is centered on the 3D and physical realm, you must now find solutions to your discomfort. Being humble enough to ask for support from others with access to more is the beginning of climbing out of this energy. You have weathered many storms before. Acknowledge your strength as you overcome this period of winter.

Connect to the Five of Pentacles

The body and nervous system can feel very dysregulated when we are depleted. Try box breathing to come back to your center. It's a four-part breath that is effective and hard to forget. So no matter how overwhelmed you're feeling, it's a tool you can use in moments of stress without adding uncertainty to your practice.

To try it . . .

1. Exhale all the stale air from your lungs, clearing out your body.

2. On your next intentional inhale, breathe in for a count of four.

3. Hold your breath for a count of four.

4. Exhale for four counts.

5. Hold at the bottom of your breath, remaining empty, for four counts.

6. Repeat a few times, or as long as needed.

Deeper Reflection

Create a powerful personal affirmation to carry you through the toughest circumstances and hardest times. Use the prompt below to fill in exactly what will give you strength:

"I am not [broken, forgotten, unworthy, losing]. I am [resilient, gifted, worthy, intentional]. I will reconnect to my inner strength now because . . ."

In My Body | Six of Pentacles

"What would you like to do when you grow up?"

"I'd like to create a space, a place, something,
   where girls can come and feel good about
      themselves,"
was my answer back then.

Years later,
I'm still pushing myself to create and form
   circles and spaces
for women to do just that.

Keywords: Generosity, Receiving, Sharing, Charity, Community support, Energetic balance of give and take, An offer

Meaning

This card is charitable and giving. If we were to define it simply, it's about providing, supporting, and sharing with others. After the difficulty of the Five of Pentacles, the next card in the earthly cycle brings us the helping hands we need. The Six of Pentacles has a more dynamic meaning now that I've developed my relationship with the tarot. I encourage all tarot readers to start to recognize something in this card. In the Rider-Waite-Smith deck, the "giver" holds coins to donate in one hand and a scale that's balanced evenly in the other. Are we more balanced than we realize? At some point along the way, the compassionate giver in this card needed help too. We all have rotated between periods of lack and plenty. When this card comes up, challenge yourself to notice which position you're in right now. Is it a time to give or receive? If you're longing to see more abundance, money, success, or *anything* in your life, Spirit might be hinting that in order to get it, it's time to surrender. Give to receive.

Notice how life could open for you more and appear more expansive if the energy and frequency of stuff, money, and resources was reciprocal, moving simultaneously toward you and away from you in balance.

Connect to the Six of Pentacles

Be of service. The most giving souls are the ones filled with purpose. When was the last time you offered your help, services, or time *just because?* Maybe volunteer for an organization or donate to a cause. It could be as simple as calling a distant friend to make sure they're doing OK or sending a gift or note via snail mail to tell a family member you're thinking of them. This tarot theme has a generous spirit and holds no ego. Don't give for the sake of getting some pat on the back for being a Good Samaritan—that's icky. Don't give because you pity others. Lean into this card with humility, giving because you know what it feels like to be in need of a helping hand.

Deeper Reflection

In contrast to your acts of service, explore your relationship with people-pleasing or holding a "savior" role. Journal about the people you show up for and the way they reciprocate (or don't). Then go a few layers deeper in this healing. Write and reflect:

- Am I a people pleaser?
- If so, when and why did that behavior start?
- What am I worthy of receiving without feeling like I have to give something first?

In My Body | Seven of Pentacles

The body knows.
It knows right from wrong.
It knows when to stay and when to go.

It knows fertile ground.
It knows where
it's worth growing roots
and sprouting flowers.

Keywords: Planning, Contemplation, Cultivation, Reflection, Assessment of a cycle thus far, Conscious effort, Persistence

Meaning

Notice when you're moving and responding to life on autopilot.

This card typically depicts a man who has toiled in the fields for what the reader can assume has been quite some time, and the seven gold pentacles gathered below him almost mock his efforts, saying "That's all you've got?" This card is our chance to keep plugging along or look elsewhere for the abundance we thought we were promised. To put it plainly, this card challenges us to weigh the pros and cons, to consider the work and if it's worth it.

Think about how many times you've faced this lesson before because it's actually quite common. A relationship hits a rocky spot, and both parties need to consider if their love is strong enough to progress or if this is a logical time to call it quits. Maybe the generous pay at a new job won't outweigh the poor work-life balance or toxic culture among coworkers. I always read this card as a chance to not only evaluate, but to redirect if needed. Remove emotion from the equation, as the practicality of the earth element is a better tool to rely on when making this judgment call. Your body can also be a compass. Ask if the level of exhaustion and tedious work you might be facing feels sustainable.

Connect to the Seven of Pentacles

Stop multitasking. This energy here is redundant and routine, and the best way to understand the message of this card is to become fully present with it. When you feel cloudy in the head and you're trying to determine what you want, keeping yourself busy will only keep you in the rut.

Another way to connect with the physicality of this card is through mindful and intentional movement. Mindful movement could mean going for a walk without a phone or doing your typical workout without music, honoring only your breath. Move a little bit slower, think through each step of your day, and observe your thoughts as you go along.

Deeper Reflection

In your journal, write seven areas of your life where you carry responsibility. Then for each, write about if you're proud of these responsibilities, if they bring you a sense of fulfillment, and why or why not.

In My Body | Eight of Pentacles

To heal is to find beauty
in the dirty fingernails,

The ones with soil tucked under them,
On the hands clutching the stems
of freshly grown and picked flowers.

To heal is to appreciate
the effort as much as
the gift.

Keywords: Mastery, Dedication, Complete attention, Finishing what you've started, Giving your best efforts, Unrelenting focus, Craftsmanship, Impeccable execution

Meaning

You've been plugging along through this Pentacles cycle and perhaps thinking to yourself, *Seriously, is the hard work going to pay off yet?* If this card came to you, I'd like to say yes (or you're getting very, very close). The complete focus and dedication of this card is what's most beautiful and admirable about it. Tactful and careful, it shows the efforts of an honest and dependable craftsman focusing on his work. If hustle culture could be summed up in one of the seventy-eight tarot cards, the Eight of Pentacles would be it. It's the grind.

While tiring yourself to the point of exhaustion shouldn't necessarily be the goal, occasionally it's what it takes. And you did *choose* to remain loyal to this work after all. (Remember that lesson and reflection in the Seven of Pentacles?) The reward will be your expertise and skill at the end of the effort. When the Eight of Pentacles shows up, it's because *you* have shown up. You're working wholeheartedly toward something you believe in. You've probably been at it for a while. You're probably great at it, or at least way better than you give yourself credit for.

While this energy is respectable, be mindful of overworking or defining yourself by your professional achievements alone.

Connect to the Eight of Pentacles

Outline a daily morning or evening routine you want to stick with for the next eight days. Make it accessible but challenging enough that you'll need to think about and consciously choose it day by day. Maybe you go the extra mile and use a trackable spreadsheet that's color-coordinated—whatever works for you! Create some discipline, channel this Eight of Pentacles energy, and notice if you can build natural momentum and focus in just eight days.

Deeper Reflection

Connect with and speak to your future self with the following prompt:

"Dear Future Me: Today, I made the necessary efforts. I stayed true to the process. I made us proud. Let me share with you, Future Self, how proud of you I am . . ."

In My Body | Nine of Pentacles

I watched my guides hand me fruits—
Cherries, strawberries, melons,
All of them pigmented
A spectrum of rich and feminine colors.
I ask them why they wish to make this offering.
"Because life is so sweet,
And because it is time to taste and savor
*   your bounty."*

Keywords: Fulfillment, Independence, Self-reliance, Physical beauty, Luxury, Affluence, Self-indulgence, Self-care, Financial achievements, Sustaining resources

Meaning

You did it. Pause now and re-read that. *You* did it. Only you.

Sit with that accomplishment and appreciate your independence. You've clearly done something right if the Nine of Pentacles is bringing this luxurious and affluent energy your way. Having worked hard, patiently and loyally committing to a process for seasons (if not years), you've collected resources you likely won't lose. There should be no doubt about what you deserve.

Self-worth is established over time, and doesn't it feel good to stand in such *knowing?* Like the figure in this card who places her hand on top of the nine grounded pentacles, we can and should be proud of the independence and self-assurance this card brings. If you're looking to earn more cash, this is a great omen. If you're wondering if you're set up for more abundance, I'd say you are. You are resting more now. The Pentacles suit asks us to carry, do, and commit relentlessly with our bodies, and finally the Nine of Pentacles brings good health, wealth, and pride, allowing us to take a well-deserved break.

Connect to the Nine of Pentacles

Invest in yourself, your body, and your comfort. Because the Pentacles is a suit of follow-through, we're not accepting excuses here. Drop any guilt about treating yourself. Whatever your version of shameless self-care looks like, go all in! For some, it's a quick session of retail therapy. For others, it might be solitude and time away to completely immerse yourself in rest for a day or two. Don't wait for a windfall of generosity or an invitation to come from someone else! You have tirelessly shown up for yourself, so you deserve this reward now. Drop your responsibilities for a moment and do something that feels nourishing for your body and spirit.

Deeper Reflection

In your journal, complete the following prompts:

- I feel most independent when I . . .

- I care and provide for myself by . . .

In My Body | Ten of Pentacles

At sixteen years old I got a bird tattooed on my
    left wrist,
chosen rashly and completely uninspired.
"What's the meaning?" others would ask me for
    years following.

Detached from my body at the time, I thought
    nothing of the choice,
ignorant to the idea that history was writing
    itself for me,
and my body was just the vehicle to land me in
the right place,
at the right time.

"There is no meaning,"

I'd answer.

At twenty-nine I watched the man I love identify birds in his parents'
        backyard up North.
"Look, another rare one! We're in luck today," he assured me.

Not long after, I took myself into meditation.
I saw her
and saw him.
I saw all of us.

I asked Spirit for her name.
"Ava," she replied.
A name I'd never thought of or considered.
As random as the bird etched into my supple skin.

I Googled the origin later.
"Birdlike, lively."

At thirty-one I sit and write this book from our deck,
A space where we live and love as two, for now.
A ring now circles my left ring finger, adorning and accessorizing the same
        arm as
my tattooed wrist.

And a bird that frequents me here perches itself on the ledge,
just feet from me.

Lucky we are, yes.
Lucky we've landed in the safety of each other
as we commit to a future with generations to come.
Lucky that it all means something now.

Keywords: Satisfaction, Affluence, Family, Ancestry, A stable home, Wealth, Tradition, Privilege, A sturdy foundation, Roots, Legacy

Meaning

The Ten of Pentacles feels hectic, busy, and *full*. This isn't a coincidence. From an art perspective, there's a lot going on. There are details filling every corner of the card's imagery. From children and loyal pets to elders and a community, *everyone* feels the security and abundance spilling out. Its tone and ties are traditional and, dare I say it, occasionally stuffy and materialistic. Think "old money" vibes. But the card revolves around fulfillment and family; therefore, it's generous, wholesome, and pure in intention.

Taking a more modern and varied approach to what wealth means to everyone, I do want to mention that there are ways to feel safe, secure, loved, and nurtured without so much *stuff*. Capitalism's influence aside, family and an established community is the basis of this card. It has a way of sharing and providing for our families, and it feels satisfying. There's a sense of peace and health within the physical body. Once we reach a finale in the tarot cycle, we hold so much of the associated element, and here, the earth element represents the strength and power of all things physical. If creating a sustainable stream of income or finding the partner who you can truly build a legacy with is your goal, this energy feels rich and supportive of those desires. If you draw this card, you could already be well on your way toward a future built on hard work, love, and commitment.

Connect to the Ten of Pentacles

Define and envision what you'd like your legacy to look like. (And before you stress out, know this is flexible! It changes, grows, and develops over time.) But right now, what do you want for yourself and your long-term future? Beyond what you need day to day, what do you wish to inspire or create in this world? How can your seemingly small presence be considered a gift to many? Take some space to imagine this, perhaps by closing your eyes and envisioning a lasting imprint of your energy. Whose heart will it touch? What change could you make? Can you challenge yourself to dream bigger or love more deeply? Trust that each and every one of us is unique and special enough to create something important, abundant, and meaningful in this lifetime.

Deeper Reflection

It's been a long cycle, and it's time to thank your body now. Through evolving seasons of arduous work and joyful miracles, your body stuck by you. Create some space in your day for the following somatic practice:

1. Choose an area of your body that brings up insecurity, and place your hands there.

2. Breathe and communicate with that space. What do you feel (physically and emotionally) when you hold it? How is the body speaking to you as you take time to honor it? Could you be more kind and loving to this part of you?

3. Write and reflect: "Thank you, body, for . . ."

PAGE of PENTACLES.

In My Body | Page of Pentacles

When I close my eyes to connect and search for answers,
all I see is green.

A field of sprawling grass,
fresh blades of promise.
Immediately I'm greeted with a sense of freedom and expansion.
It's here where I become a student of my own soul.

Character Traits: Serious, Tactful, Helpful, A perfectionist, An apprentice, A future leader, Supportive, Curious, Opportunistic

Meaning

This Page is longing for you to look at the world with childlike wonder and marvel at all the opportunities that await you. It's certainly a messenger of fruitful new beginnings, similar to the Ace of Pentacles but with an even more eager spirit and a willingness to take on any challenge. When this card presents itself in your reading, you can absolutely lean into any hobbies and interests, professional endeavors, or possibilities nearby. With grounded feet and a willing and able body, the Page of Pentacles can remind us that sometimes the best way of learning something new is by trying it. Use the body mindfully and discover how capable you are, even if that means encountering some mistakes or scuffing your knees along the way as you experience the occasional misstep or mistake.

Channel the Page of Pentacles

Invite in a new vibration through free movement. Movement is incredibly healing because it shakes up and shakes off energies that remain dense in your physical body. This card feels opportunistic and excited, so mimic this excitement by bringing movement to your body, which will make you feel more alive and in tune with what could come your way next.

Start by standing and placing your feet firmly against the ground. Keeping the remainder of your body soft and balanced, freely *shake*! This can look like shrugging your shoulders or rapidly bending each knee back and forth. It can look like swinging your arms up and down and left and right. It can look like wiggling in your fingers or shimmying your hips wildly and eventually hopping around a bit. Let every limb vibrate in motion with no destination, just moving to move. Notice how your breath quickens and your spirit feels more activated the longer you do this. Notice how revved up and excited you feel to simply be standing, moving, and being in your physical container.

Deeper Reflection

Complete these lists:

- These are some of the places, habits, hobbies, and ideas I hope to explore someday . . .

- Here are parts of myself I'm learning, the parts of me that I'm not completely familiar with, but remain curious about . . .

In My Body | Knight of Pentacles

To do anything,

The work,
The pleasure,
The pain,

Without love,
is to do it without life.

Character traits: Active, Dependable, A team player, Patient, Protective, Calming, Professional, Focused, Traditional, A purist, Stubborn, Proud, Stable, Responsible

Meaning

This card's energy moves slowly and methodically, but with patience and strength. When a Knight of Pentacles character comes your way, you might want to hire them because it's hard to imagine someone more willing or loyal to the process and more intentional with their actions and work. If this card is not representing a helpful member of your team (be it at work, in your home, or as your partner), it is your tarot deck's way of calling you toward hard work and promising you abundant results if you stay grounded. Just be mindful that your routines and efforts don't become inflexible.

As we move on a path toward our greatest potential and our higher self, there are inevitable pivot points, moments of redirection. This knight's personality doesn't do well with change or spontaneity. His natural integrity is something to be proud of and never lose sight of. Whether you're working toward a monetary goal or simply showing up for the people you love and adore, do so with integrity.

Channel the Knight of Pentacles

Declare your love and loyalty to something. Whether this is written privately in your notebook or expressed as a spoken oath of commitment that others can hold you accountable for, don't be afraid to be tied to work, people, and promises for the long haul.

What are you most loyal to? What are you ready to be more loyal to? What would these promises look like, and are you ready to make them? To the commitment-phobes: Start as small as you need. If you're not sure what to commit to, use your inner healing and personal growth as inspiration. There's always the opportunity to make a commitment to yourself. For example, you could say, "I am going to stay loyal to my healing this year and start therapy." To someone who's *really* ready to dive in, this card may inspire the type of commitment and honest effort it takes to launch their dream business, propose to the love of their life, or purchase that scary-but-rewarding investment in themselves.

Deeper Reflection

In your journal, recall some of your greatest achievements and the most laborious chapters of your life. Remember not just the tiresome work, but the fulfilling work as well.

Then write: "When I kept moving forward, when I chose not to quit or give up on myself, I felt/did . . ."

QUEEN of PENTACLES

In My Body | Queen of Pentacles

She finds God in nature
when she's marveling at the Universe—
the one she's cultivated both inside and outside
of herself.

Character Traits: Divine, Nurturing, Feminine, Intuitive, Maternal, Generous, Comfort, Stable, Resilient, Resourceful, Unafraid, Peaceful, Fertile, Limitless

Meaning

When this queen archetype sits before you in a reading, you're looking at someone with a personality and presence that feels like home. You may want to cuddle up beside her, listen to her advice, and wrap yourself in her quiet, confident presence. She brings a safety that is difficult to describe but certainly felt.

The most fascinating and dimensional part of this queen is how holistically she lives. It's like she has struck the perfect balance between family life and professional satisfaction. She's no stranger to hard work (after all, no member of the Pentacles court shies away from labor). She also knows the importance of family. Her body and home are a part of her abundance as well. She makes sure that each blessing is accounted for. She shows up to remind us that enrichment is important. This queen shares her healing through manifestation, organic and effortless worthiness, and fertility. When she meets us in a reading, we could be primed to birth our next beautiful and abundant reality. We could be feeling a pull to nurture and grow what we have, what we're investing our time into, and what we're working toward. Our goals are the priority, but our peace of mind and health won't be compromised at its expense.

Channel the Queen of Pentacles

Host a dinner party! Inviting your loved ones over for quality time in the sanctuary of your space is the most earthy (and fun!) embodiment of this queen. Make it cozy with a meal sourced close to the earth and keep the group size intimate. Use the good silverware or make a delectable mocktail to celebrate the simple gift of being alive and in the company of others. The Queen of Pentacles knows her guests deserve the best, and she's proud to offer not only her attention, but the bounty she's worked for and the space she occupies.

If hosting isn't your forte, make something for a friend or family member. Gather a bouquet of their favorite flowers, write a handwritten letter of appreciation, or knit a beanie if you're crafty. Do you, but just be sure to show your gratitude for them by making something with love.

Deeper Reflection

Take your gratitude practice a step further. Start by writing down three things you're grateful for. Easy, right? Great, now with that list in hand, come up with three actions you can take in response to these gifts.

Grateful for your grandparents? Call them. Grateful for your health? Go on a walk to celebrate your body's vitality. Grateful for your pets? Stop rushing those cuddles with them in the morning. You get the gist here. Acknowledge and nurture what already exists in your life!

KING of PENTACLES.

In My Body | King of Pentacles

When I think of my father, I think of his words.

"You're my hero."
"I'm your biggest fan."
"I love you more than anything in the world."

The same way I remember the secret handshake
I made up for us as a child
Or the way he called me each night at eight
to say goodnight.

With repetition like that,
I could never forget.

Character Traits: Sturdy, Supportive, Generous, Paternal, A provider, Traditional, Invested in himself, Stoic, Business-minded, A man of his word

Meaning

There's something stabilizing about finding this father archetype in our readings. The tarot is asking you to prioritize your healing the same way the King of Pentacles provides for himself. He commits, and he stays true to what he believes in, even if his ideals feel antiquated to others.

As a paternal court rank combined with the earth element, this personality steadies us with a supportive and affluent energy. This King knows how to generate and build an empire that's rooted in love for the work and efforts he made over the course of a lifetime. When you pull this card, notice what you're building and how you're providing for yourself and others. You may want to ask yourself what work you value and love doing so you can continue to use it to manifest the life you desire.

This card is a fantastic one to pull when you are seeking financial security, as it shows you're taking the most respectable and responsible path toward that goal. This king is a businessman and a patient and traditional figure who shows us that slow and steady can actually win the race. Our lifetime is a marathon rather than a sprint, and this patient and protective figure might be asking you as a reader to take stock of what is most important to you, invest in your health and your resources, and appreciate where you have built abundance.

This card is a steady reminder that you are valuable. Your time, skills, and love are all plentiful. The King of Pentacles may manage money well, but he's not a greedy man. He creates and encourages a legacy built by hand, then shares it through an extension of his loving heart.

Channel the King of Pentacles

Recommit to (or start) a brand-new tradition. Traditions are sacred experiences because they allow us to ingrain and savor memories over and over again. We relive something we love, choosing it repeatedly to show our appreciation for the way a memory can make us feel. The King of Pentacles is often labeled as the businessman, the money guy, the person most obsessed with success, but let us not forget his commitment to family, tradition, and his legacy. Come up with a tradition that could withstand the test of time while remaining unique and true to your family story. Because this energy is abundant, share it with others so they can practice and celebrate the tradition with you. "Family" is a circle we can draw as large as we'd like.

Deeper Reflection

In your journal, finish the following prompt:

"This is the type of world I hope to live in, and this is how my inner work leads to the reality of such a beautiful world . . ."

8

In My Emotions

THE SUIT OF CUPS

The Suit of Cups, associated with the water element, asks us to *feel*. It calls us to expose our subconscious thoughts, claim and call out our need for love and belonging, and provide forgiveness. It cleanses the psyche by bringing us to a state of emotional vulnerability. Much like a powerful body of water that is deceptively difficult to contain, this suit of emotion offers us a direct channel into a vast and sometimes other-worldly part of ourselves: our heart. It brings intention to the forefront of our awareness, asking us to feel and respond instead of merely reacting to situations that make us uncomfortable. Above everything, this element heals.

And that is why this is my favorite part of the deck and tarot experience. There are some very special cards housed in this suit. My own healing experience became most authentic when I accepted the rush of water and finally allowed its infinite intuitive power to wash over me.

When I began connecting with my spirituality, I was gathering interesting tools like tarot, but I wasn't embodying much of what they promoted. I was in a constant state of self-imposed burnout, trapped in the belief that I had to be strong in order to prove I had overcome my past traumas. I defined strength as my ability to live life by my own rules, to be the leader of my destiny for every single moment ahead of me. I (mistakenly) thought that to lose control was to fail. I was a young, determined entrepreneur and #girlboss. I often was angry and resentful, but wasn't everyone? I was dissatisfied and felt misunderstood in my relationship, but . . . that's normal, right? It turns out I was holding myself to a patriarchal misbelief that the only way to show I had risen from the ashes of my past was to stay in a constant upward, exhausting climb toward my own unrealistic expectations.

I spent that toxic phase of my life treading water (no pun intended). I was genuinely determined to heal. I knew my need for control was limiting the capacity of my life, and I knew I was being asked to go easier on myself; I just hadn't quite figured out how to do it yet.

My first ever spiritual mentor read tarot cards and had a big influence on me starting my own card-pulling practice. She was what can only be described as *witchy*. A New Yorker who had recently moved upstate to paint more, wear bras less, and provide spiritual coaching over Zoom to women trying to love themselves back together again (like me), she (also like me) was a former cigarette-smoking, easily angered hard-ass who had discovered yoga, meditation, and mindfulness and enjoyed them more than she had expected to.

The first card she ever pulled for me was the Temperance card. Looking back, I realize I probably fell in love with tarot right then and there. The message of the card made me feel something more sincere and hopeful than the other ways I was self-soothing.

While the Temperance card is not a member of the Cups suit, it is also associated with the water element. This Major Arcana archetype features a rebalancing of water between two chalices. Behind the figure depicted in the card are mountains, a nod to the hardship and challenges we've overcome in the past. It remains one of my favorite cards to teach.

When that card appeared, I knew that true self-love (not just bubble baths and affirmation sticky notes, but real, unconditional self-love) was the only thing that stood in the way of me living a balanced life with more intimate connections and relationships with others, having a deeply special and sacred relationship with my intuition, and cultivating my divine femininity with confidence. Self-love was the ticket to becoming *myself* so I could show up more authentically in the external world.

My mentor was not as overwhelmed by this realization as I was.

"Can you create balance?" she asked me, like it was the easiest thing in the world to do.

"Shit, I have no idea." I laughed. "I'm too young to stop hustling. I have a lot to prove first." This young version of me thought finding balance meant settling or giving up a life of success. I couldn't comprehend how or why someone *wouldn't* want to stick in a loop of chasing highs and shaming yourself in the lows.

My spiritual guide just smirked at me. A great mentor, like a great card reader, lets the seeker arrive at the answer on their own. And although it took me longer than I care to admit, I remember vividly when it clicked.

A couple weeks later, I was sitting with my knees curled up to my chest in the shower (a ritual that remains part of my daily routine to this day), beads of warm water running across my skin. Mindless and unattached, I was lost in a daydream. I held my hand up and noticed water droplets hitting the center of my palm, changing course, and deviating from their original path from the shower head to accommodate my body on their way to the ground.

I became extremely aware of how the drops let themselves flow where I directed them. There was no force, only ease. Rather than forcefully drilling a hole through my palm to make their way to their destination, they let themselves trickle from my fingertips, eventually landing on the floor of the shower and at last circling down the drain.

I laughed to myself from the floor of the shower. Was it really that easy? Could I, like water, move gracefully and let myself flow with compassion and flexibility to the exact same destination I was already headed? Was it possible to become the version of myself I wanted to be through a beautiful and fluid dance?

This might seem obvious, but at the time, it wasn't clear to me. Sure, I was falling in love with yoga, discovering meditation, and feeling something far bigger than myself (Spirit). But I had no funnel to channel it through or container to hold it in. I was stuck in a life of extremes, allowing myself to thrive in chaos.

It might sound silly, but seeing the Suit of Cups in action in my shower helped me see the value in this feminine element. I started to let it hold me, change me, soften me. A truly connected tarot practice requires this flexibility as well.

In this chapter, you'll find glimpses of how the water element in tarot led me to this place of self-love I now reside in. I am now on a shore of peace, looking out toward the horizon of a life where I know I am never forcing but actively cocreating it.

Suit of Cups Associations

Element: Water

Chakra: Sacral

Timing and speed: One month or moon cycle

Astrological signs: Cancer, Scorpio, Pisces

Season: Summer

The Suit of Cups is . . .

Loving, Healing, Romantic, Intuitive, Compassionate, Connected to the Subconscious, Feminine

When Reading for Yourself

Practice with intention. When we receive the soft, forgiving, and maternal energy of the Cups cards, we often feel tended to, nurtured, and held. Within this soft cocoon of emotional understanding, you may want to hunker down and rest in the space. You might not feel like doing anything or adjusting in reaction to the cards.

And that's OK. Instead, I invite you to let yourself *respond* to the messages the cards bring you. Add some contemplation to your practice. Notice where in your experiences you're beginning to shy away from the next step because it frightens you, or where you are taking the flexibility of the Cups perhaps a bit too far. Are you avoiding confrontation? Ask what aligned action would look like when supported by the generous flow of water and the Suit of Cups. Adopt a compassionate energy to complement and amplify the parts of yourself that need to be brave and proactive and take leadership of your life.

But keep in mind, the water element requires us to accept her potent but shapeless nature. While water heals, we must frequently remind ourselves that it can also drown. Let her move you, but keep your intention in your experience.

When Reading for Someone Else

Be gentle. My greatest and most consistent advice to tarot readers who are presenting the themes of the Cups is to soften their tone to ease the body and embrace the energy of the person across from them. This is our energetic way of offering them assurance while diving into topics that can be sensitive: "You're okay to be who you are, right here, right now."

Shedding a tear, getting vulnerable, and sharing our story is an act of intimacy and is never easy in front of other people. Combining that act of bravery with a stack of cards can feel like the emotional equivalent of Russian roulette. Those who come to you for readings are naturally going to be unsure if their greatest hopes and dreams or their deepest wounds (or both!) will show up in the cards. They sit across from you, exposed, as you share themes like ego death, defensiveness, greed, grief, and self-sabotage that run freely through the seventy-eight archetypes. It would take a pretty disconnected person to not have some feeling of vulnerability in that situation.

Soften yourself for them. Bring a soothing tone to your voice and a gentleness to your eyes. Show how loving and beautiful these cards can be. Let your card descriptions be passionate. Let the tarot offer them a love letter, and show them the beauty of this suit by simply holding space for them. Listen just as much as you speak when reading the Cups. Be poetic in your presentation.

Tip: Put simply, remember to be kind in your readings! With the number of distractions and notifications we are inundated with all day, it's a blessing and a gift to be heard, seen, and fully celebrated for everything we feel, have felt, and continue to yearn for from an open and authentic heart. This is not the space to overanalyze or get stuck in your logical mind as a reader.

Tarot Outside of the Deck

In life and in your tarot practice, follow what sends shivers down your spine. Gravitate toward what triggers deep gratitude and appreciation. Notice the people, places, and experiences that bring tears of joy to your eyes. When I'm channeling for myself or a particularly open client, asking Spirit and my cards for messages that speak to the heart and soul experience, I tend to cry. Not a guttural sob (although there would be nothing wrong with that!) but a soft and subtle release. Catharsis.

I can identify it. When it happens to me, I sit quietly in it, present and in amazement of how my body can hold an ocean of emotion and universal energy, knowing this is the magic of my psychic experience.

Exercise

Romanticize your life and spiritual practice. Not every chapter of spiritual growth has to feel full of shadow or density. Spirituality can be beautiful; in fact, it's meant to. So set aside any fear of looking like you're straight out of a rom-com and let yourself literally dance in the rain. Immerse yourself in water to receive an energetic hydration. Finding joy in these moments is the only way to sustain this deep and transformational work.

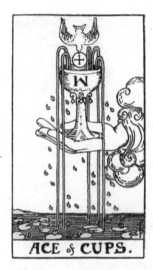

ACE ᴏꜰ CUPS.

In My Emotions | Ace of Cups

Sitting on the floor of the shower, I bow my
head as the droplets kiss my crown.
They rush down my face, dance off the tip of
my nose.
I close my eyes and imagine light pouring in.
Already in this space to cleanse, I take it a step
further,
receiving what feels like an energetic baptism
each time.

Keywords: A fresh cycle in love and healing, Self-love, Purity, Cleansing, A heart-centered gift from Spirit, A clear new beginning

Meaning

When this card arrives, I feel both comforted and connected to myself. The intention behind it is so pure; it's like the Universe's way of drying our tears and giving us hope again after moving through an emotional cycle. It suggests a feeling of peace, when we have invested enough time into our healing that we actually embody what those inspiring Instagram quotes preach about: self-love. The Ace of Cups floods us with a fresh opportunity (and perspective) around love, emotional healing, and intimacy. It asks where you'll direct this flow of compassionate, kind, and beautifully vulnerable energy. The river of love is vast and available to you at this moment. You may channel it toward someone, but I suggest you fill your cup first. This card is sensitive and sacred. It holds the gentle power of divine femininity you can use to cleanse, support, and nurture how you see fit. Allow love to be simple. Stay soft and open. This is your invitation into your own heart.

Connect to the Ace of Cups

Get in touch with water, literally. Whether connecting to it in nature, drawing a bath, or taking a moment to sip fruit-infused water, *feel* it.

Dip your toes in a body of water as often as you can. Play in puddles you pass as you walk home. Notice the way water supports and holds you, no matter the form.

Deeper Reflection
Write a love letter to yourself. Continue to write past the discomfort and awkwardness you may feel when doing this, and let words spill onto your page. Write like you are confessing your love to someone you deeply care for.

In My Emotions | Two of Cups

They warn you that love requires compromise,
*   yet it always felt like a sacrifice to me,*
Until I looked up and found those eyes level
*   with mine.*
Present and promising, but not interfering
*   with the view of my chosen path,*
He was right there, matching me, choosing me.

Keywords: Conscious connection, Loyal beginnings, Partnership, A heart-centered choice, Showing up for another, Balance, Feeling intuitively guided in relationships and emotional state

Meaning

The Two of Cups is a card of connection and loyalty that symbolizes the honest effort to prioritize companionship and care for someone outside of yourself. While it often represents the union of two souls on a romantic journey, it can also transcend love stories and mark collaborations or friendships with soul-driven and heart-led people—those we were fated to meet and learn from.

Whether you subscribe to the notion of soulmates or trust in the magic of serendipitous meetups, these relationships consist of the people who quickly become supporting roles in our journey and hold space in our fondest memories.

The Two of Cups captures our instinct to walk a vulnerable path alongside another. With this card, two forces meet in perfect unison. In a singular moment (it's never promised forever), their vibrations match. My favorite part of this card is the balance and reciprocation of both parties. They connect physically at the very center of the card to show the reader that they came from different directions but are now together, standing as one in the same space.

I also love to explore the mirrors of partnership in this card. Is it possible that the Two of Cups can represent two sides of ourselves, one reflecting back at us? Our past selves? Our future selves? We can rely on tarot to be most potent when we ask about personal healing or partake in independent experiences. Let yourself accept and reflect on the duality of this card.

Connect to the Two of Cups

Practice touch. Remember that physical contact isn't just a love language, but a basic human need. It can also be given to and received by ourselves. Who says you can't massage your own feet after a long day? If you have someone—platonic or romantic—who's willing to hold your hand during a difficult conversation or carve a space on their shoulder for you to rest on, take them up on the offer.

Deeper Reflection

Take a few moments to consider who holds the space as the closest relationship in your life. Who do you consider your closest confidante? This is the soul you give the most to in terms of attention, affection, and emotional space. Through a soft gaze, or with eyes closed, access a meditative space and imagine them across from you. How close are they, really? Do they stand in the middle, balancing you? Are the scales even? Take your intuitive awareness a step further. Can you energetically sense any blocks from them toward you? Notice the subtle or obvious differences between the two of you.

In My Emotions | Three of Cups

After a couple tequila sodas,
With cheese dangling from my chin
Thanks to a savior disguised as a slice of pizza,
I am reminded that I am human.
And then I notice my friends around me, with
     their matching grease-stained lips,
Choosing to witness the human I'm willing
     to be.

Keywords: Authentic friendships, The family we create, Joyful celebration and shared experiences, Sisterhood and brotherhood, Sacred bonds

Meaning

You know those moments when you find yourself belly laughing with your closest friends over a tasty margarita (or a slice of extra cheesy pizza)? Maybe the weather is perfect, the sun has just set, and you're reminiscing about similar evenings in the past? A sequence of hilarious stories and playful banter keep the flow of conversation as endless as the drinks. That's how I'd describe idyllic Three of Cups moments. This card is communal and encourages the simple celebration of life.

The Three of Cups describes relationships with people who show up for us without hesitation. They want to bask in the glory of our achievements and highest highs, and they would never miss our party. When these friends gather it's almost guaranteed to be fun, carefree, and effortless. There's an understanding that only time and true intimacy can provide. These are connections that must be cherished endlessly.

This card doesn't just represent our friendships; it also represents our safest community. Any member of our circle, including our spiritual circle (Spirit Guides and ancestors), can earn a spot in this card's experience.

Consider this the crew who doesn't expect anything of you. With them, you feel you can release the expectations of how you *should* be, as your imperfections are what attracted their love for you in the first place.

Connect to the Three of Cups
Express vulnerability to a friend you trust, let a hug last a couple of seconds longer, send an appreciative text message, or allow direct eye contact to linger. Show up for others in a way that honors how they show up for you.

Deeper Reflection
Write and reflect:

- What does the word "sisterhood/brotherhood" mean to me?
- What do my sacred bonds provide for me that I wouldn't be able to cultivate alone?
- How does the beauty I see in each of them mirror the beauty I hold within myself?

In My Emotions | Four of Cups
Is this avoidance or dissatisfaction?
It feels like avoidance.
Because if I looked into the eyes of someone I
*   loved deeply,*
I would never tell them to delay or settle.

Keywords: Stagnancy, Apathy and indifference, Lack of inspiration, Monotony

Meaning

The Four of Cups shows boredom, an unwelcome energy of apathy after the previous joy surrounding the Two and Three of Cups. But all good things must come to an end, right?

While the Four of Cups isn't overtly negative, it is uncomfortably safe. It's like living on autopilot, unamused and unbothered by much, and therefore unsure where to invest your heart space or emotions next. It's where the elemental energy of water stabilizes (fours in tarot are always stabilizing) into a state that can be described as . . . blah. Our emotions are deep pools that can bring endlessly vast highs and lows, and constantly swinging back and forth in those extremes is downright exhausting. As a reader, receiving this card can remind you that it's important to sit and reflect on your emotional experience instead of letting yourself be constantly pulled by its tides.

Ask yourself, *Am I safe in this boredom right now? How can I find space for emotional equilibrium?* A gray emotional space serves us until it doesn't. Intuitively we must also decide if that apathy is teetering on a lack of gratitude or fulfillment. Is there more to explore and demand of ourselves? Are we settling for surface-level introspection?

Connect to the Four of Cups

Before trying to access a deeper layer of the emotional body that doesn't feel present or genuine, shake off the lackluster debris of whatever is causing this apathy and indifference. You don't even have to name or reconcile the blah-ness to release it.

Try the Breath of Joy to move past the Four of Cups. This is my favorite breathwork technique to come back to myself and my energy through cathartic release.

1. Come to stand with your feet about hip-width apart. Bring a soft bend to your knees and let your arms hang loosely to begin. On your inhale, breathe into your nose in three parts, taking three tiny sips of air until you reach the top

of your breath. On your exhale, release completely with a large sigh from your mouth.

2. Now, add movement. Create a T shape with your arms on your first inhale, spreading your fingertips wide. On your second inhale, draw your arms straight up like you're reaching for the sky. On your third inhale, let them sweep back down to find that T shape, extending out long from your side body.

3. Let your exhale bring you release. Relax your head and neck, bend at your knees, and drape your arms down so they can graze the ground. The bend in your knees is deep and gentle here. You're surrendering stagnancy and dropping in with each exhale, reinviting and experiencing fresh *prana* and joy on each inhale. You'll feel buzzy and alive the longer you practice this. Bring your hands to your body (one hand on your belly, one hand on your heart) whenever you need to pause and reconnect.

Deeper Reflection

Pick a song you love, one that makes you *feel* something! In your journal, reflect on the following prompt and write for one complete song: "These are the spaces (in my environment, relationships, and hobbies) where I notice myself feeling more awakened, more challenged, more inspired, more alive . . ."

In My Emotions | Five of Cups

First slowly and stealthily, so smooth I could
*   have mistaken myself as the one running.*
Then suddenly a sprint! You were gone.
It's here in this emptiness that I learn what
*   grief actually feels like.*

Keywords: Heaviness, Sadness, Grief
and mourning, Abandonment, Regret,
Isolation and loneliness, Separation

Meaning

I associate this card with emptiness in the heart
space. Here and there we face circumstances
we didn't plan for, and we're left carrying a weight our bodies, hearts, and
souls haven't been trained to handle just yet. Somehow, we muster the
strength and resilience to hold the experience and push through.

While this card is burdensome, there's an inevitable dawn that awaits
once we pass this threshold of pain at the middle of the ace-to-ten cycle.
While it's uncomfortable to rest in, the Five of Cups signifies that peace
and opportunity will come when the tears have dried. But for now, the
well of emotion is deep and it's difficult to see the bottom. Resist the
urge to judge this human experience.

Connect to the Five of Cups

Feel. The practice here is simply to feel and ride each emotional wave of
the circumstance you are going through. While there's a good chance
you didn't choose this Five of Cups energy, there's an undeniable need
to surrender to it. Your task here is to simply allow your feelings to
swell and sweep through your energetic body whenever you think about
the subject. Let a tear drop without resistance. Know that the only way
out of the darkness is through. In terms of the trajectory of our story
and soul's path, these are the valleys we occasionally fall into after (and
before) the peaks.

Deeper Reflection

In your journal, create two lists. Use the first to describe all the spaces, people, and moments you mourn in some way. In the second list, write down all the reasons why it's acceptable to feel this way right now.

In My Emotions | Six of Cups

Seek to hear the voices of your ancestors.
Explore the night sky to find them.
Gaze in wonder at their radiance.
Call out to them and hear the resounding
*   echoes that follow.*
Pull from the voices of those not here to speak
*   for themselves.*
Heal on behalf of your lifetimes before.

Keywords: Purity, Innocence, Childhood, Memories, Nostalgia, Past lifetimes

Meaning

A sweet and nostalgic energy greets us with warmth and sincerity at this point in the cycle. This is a card that can be taken in many directions. At its core there's a clear representation of the past, and we have intuitive liberty to read how that past is influencing or encouraging our present actions. Like the image depicted on the card of a young child gifting a flower they picked, we can find the beauty in small gestures, the little things that were always profound and *enough* before life got more complicated, overburdened, adult-like, and serious. Our inner children, our innocence, and our past lives are all represented in the Six of Cups. The card could signify a literal journey back to a place or person we've known or grown up around, or it could point to previous lifetimes your soul can vaguely recall.

Connect to the Six of Cups

Do something childish today. If connecting with a very young version of you feels uncomfortable, decide on an age that brings nostalgia and piques your interest. (For me, that's my teenage self. I find her hilarious and often delusional, but strong in her own way.) Then engage with them. Listen to the music you blasted out the windows of your first car or cook the not-so-nutritious recipe you and your roommate devoured too often in college. Do something that brings up a memory of when life was imperfectly perfect.

Deeper Reflection

Explore your thoughts on what it means to be naïve. How comfortable are you not knowing something? Do you feel resistant, uncomfortable, exposed? Write to a point where you begin to affirm that naivety and innocence are synonymous with openness, softness, and childlike curiosity.

In My Emotions | Seven of Cups

Our souls have experienced more than our
  bodies,
Yet the body carries every experience and gives
  it a home.
No wonder some emotions and reactions feel
  intrusive, unfamiliar, dissociative . . .
Like strangers.

Keywords: Disassociation, Skewed emotional lens, Many choices, Disconnection, Illusion, Imagination, Ungrounded emotional state, Uncertainty around opportunities, Overwhelm, Wishful thinking

Meaning

Likely the most complex and difficult of the Cups cards, this energy brings a cloudiness and unease that feels anything but grounded. It's as if we're staring into the abyss of opportunities and our imagination and uncertainty is getting the best of us. What is real versus imaginary? Where is my true longing and desire? What do I really want from my life? From my relationships? From myself? Am I pretending? I mention in previous chapters that the sevens point to self-awareness, and this card is no different.

Traditionally the figure represented in the imagery isn't a figure at all; it's a black silhouette staring at seven overflowing cups in the void in front of them. Ask yourself, *Who am I in this experience I'm living? Have I lost touch?* Take this opportunity to turn the answer back toward your truth. In the process of trying to keep up, find purpose and develop connection, sometimes we unconsciously disassociate from our heart space in a way that only self-inquiry can remedy. If this card finds you, slow down and unplug. Do less. With this card I always use the metaphor of a buffet. You arrive starving and gluttonous, ready to indulge in all the dishes and options, overwhelmed but opportunistic. You're stuffed not long after this, desensitized to flavor. Yet oddly you want more sensation, somehow squeezing in dessert.

Don't get me wrong, having choices in front of us is exciting, enticing, and occasionally necessary, but there is such a thing as distraction and avoidance. The answer you were seeking for so long may be shrouded in multiple paths and options, but trust me, your heart already knows it.

Connect to the Seven of Cups

Declutter, socially and physically. Take a break from social media, be mindful of how many commitments you're making on your calendar, and spend fifteen to twenty minutes today decluttering a space where you deserve mental and emotional rest, like your bedroom or creative workspace.

Deeper Reflection

In your journal, re-ground yourself with seven simple lines of personal truths. Start each line with "I know . . ."

For example: "I know I'm a loving and kind person. I know I'm deserving of relationships and energies that reciprocate."

In My Emotions | Eight of Cups

The day has come for me to let go.
I hope you know I held on tirelessly.

Keywords: Surrender, Disconnection, Emotional release, Empowered withdrawal, Walking away, Leaving behind a difficult situation, Courage, Emotional strength

Meaning

This card presents itself when we begin to walk away. We have invested a great deal of time and effort into a person, goal, or place, but the cons list finally extends so far past the pros that we cannot make excuses anymore. The lesson of this card carries the white flag we wave when we realize what has not, and will never, fulfill us completely. We outgrow it. We heal. This growth is not due to someone else's efforts; it's all you. That's my favorite part about this card: it's a self-empowered and completely independent choice. We're often still weary and emotionally raw during these Eight of Cups lessons, feeling disconnected and in a period of transition, but we are sure of ourselves and our ability to discover more depth and joy. Remember that this self-assurance and certainty is a superpower during this vulnerable chapter. That self-assurance is strength.

Connect to the Eight of Cups

Sit comfortably and ground your physical body. Bring your palms together and gently rub them together. Close your eyes and visualize, in between your palms, what you'd like to disconnect from. Place your left hand on your heart and extend your right palm out in front of you. Draw your palms back together to generate more heat and energy. Repeat the motion and reset. This movement clears the energetic cord and releases you from the source of your discomfort. Rub your palms together again, moving and restating the separation. Repeat the following phrases to yourself:

- "This is mine [left hand to heart], and this is theirs [right arm and hand extend out]."
- "This is what I'm willing to hold, and this is what I am not."
- "I am here, and this energy is there."

Do this as many times as necessary to feel the disconnect.

Deeper Reflection

Using the following prompt, connect with and speak to your future self: "I'd like to share with you, Future Self, how good life is going to get . . ."

Consider your response a proclamation that you will dedicate yourself to the practice of continually surrendering to (and trusting) your future self. Make a promise to yourself that you'll continue seeking the fulfillment you long for!

In My Emotions | Nine of Cups

Spirit and your guides want you to know your
dreams are valid,
Even if you are simply dreaming of a feeling.

Keywords: Emotional fulfillment,
Joy, Celebration, Wishes granted,
Satisfaction, Success and achievements

Meaning

This card connects us to a joyful moment
and authentic sense of pride. It's not a
forceful pride that's loud and obvious. No,
this card is not boastful. Instead, this is a
pride that extends the aura and can be felt from others who pass you
on the street or bump into you at the coffee shop.

"Wow, they have a great *vibe*," they might say.

And how did you get so *vibey*, you ask? You followed what made you
feel emotionally fulfilled. You patiently floated down the lazy river (or
swam against the difficult current) of the Cups cycle. Through the lows,
confusions, and now peaceful highs of the process, you led with your
heart, intuition, and compassion. You discovered the true meaning of
life: contentment.

The Nine of Cups usually brings a payoff. It usually holds a gift, manifestation, or wish fulfillment that makes this card pretty hard to beat. It
instills a sense of pride and fulfillment that allows us to rest (traditionally
the figure on the card is seated) and receive from the universal support
we've earned. It's also a party card. Celebration and cheers are in order!
The most profound aspect of this card is the fact that the figure is usually
shown alone. This is a beautiful experience when shared with others, but
it is just as beautiful when you throw that party for yourself.

Connect to the Nine of Cups

Have a "me day." This is a trend in the self-help and self-improvement spaces that I, as an extreme introvert, am *very* aligned with.

The concept of a "me day" revolves around spending an entire day doing exactly what is going to bring the most joy. From breakfast to the last moment of your nightly routine, you dress, move, eat, enjoy, and support yourself exactly the way your soul craves. You make choices that provide for you on such an emotional level that you can't help but feel the type of satisfaction that radiates and makes each moment feel like a core memory.

It's not selfish to fill our cups first. In fact, it's necessary before you can receive the forever fantasy you're striving for in the Nine of Cups. Feeling satisfaction and pride with your achievements and blessings, rather than asking for more, is a beautiful feeling of ease and contentment that deserves celebrating.

Deeper Reflection

Let's do a take on a gratitude list. Respond to this prompt: "Where have I witnessed Spirit and the Universe show up for me?"

Write until you feel complete and reconnected to your joy. Following that list, explore further and bring your tarot knowledge to your writing: "What experiences, memories, and specific cards/chapters of the journey did I witness to get to this place?"

Tip: Stay patient with yourself if any part of this reflection is challenging. Learning all seventy-eight cards by memory takes time. As you evolve in your practice, you'll find yourself identifying "card moments" or glimpses of times and situations you can associate the name of a card with. You're a tarot reader from the first time you pick up a deck, but you'll feel like a more seasoned and legitimate reader when you start applying the cards in real life, seeing them living and breathing around you.

In My Emotions | Ten of Cups

In meditation today I found myself by my
   mother's herb garden,
The one she planted beyond the door of the
   screened-in porch.
I typically avoid returning to this home in my
   memories,
But my inner child grabbed my hand and led
   me there.

She started dancing,
Proud of her floral dress and matching
   headband.
Her mousy brown bob swayed in a similar
   fashion to the hem of her dress.

But then I noticed my parents,
And they didn't look like how I remember them back then.
They looked calm. Without stress. No anger.
They were fixated on me.

While I danced, they cheered me on.
As an outsider observing the family, I felt overjoyed.
To watch my parents celebrate their five-year-old rather than terrorize each
   other or sabotage themselves was one of the most healing experiences I'd
   ever had in meditation.
Right there, by the herb garden.

Keywords: Happiness, Bliss, Healed connections, Harmony, Security, Emotional safety, Healthy families, Stable and abundant homes, Homecomings, Stable relationships, Long-term partnerships, Blessings

Meaning

Traditionally, this card sets the stage for a "white picket fence" lifestyle—the dog, the kids, the cute and cozy cottage in the distance. It means well, I'll admit. But it's hardly inclusive, and it's not aligned with more modern lifestyle choices that question and break free from a societal standard reminiscent of our grandparents' generation.

Looking past the traditional and antiquated depiction of happiness, and looking instead at the energetic and emotional components of this card, we can find a sense of harmony, safety in the home, and a healing that radiates from the chosen family unit to our communities—an abundance of love so powerful it can transcend and uplift others who have not quite found it yet. Let's face it: don't we need those representations of what's possible in order to continue feeling committed to the healing? We like to applaud and admire all sorts of success stories, like the blissfully married elderly couple that is welcoming a great-grandchild to their family or the pregnant woman overjoyed that her trials with infertility finally paid off.

We are constantly working hard on ourselves to make peace with and forgive our pasts. The Ten of Cups reminds us not to limit what's possible for our futures. It allows us to trust that deep gratitude, wish fulfillment, and happily-ever-afters are not just theories used to sell romantic comedies or persuade us to try new dating sites or invest in overpromising life coaching programs. We know in our hearts what will be authentic in our hearts and feel like *home*. Our ideal lives, whether that includes the white picket fence or fancy hybrid SUV to drive our kids to soccer practice or not, can be created, manifested, and determined by us.

Connect to the Ten of Cups

Drop into your meditation practice and create a safe space for you and your inner child. When you're ready, invite your inner child to join you. Play with them. Ask them what they fear and what they enjoy. Have an honest conversation with them. I've learned through my intuitive work to let them guide the conversations. They are often wiser than we are in some ways. Respond in the most affirming and responsible tone you can. You can imagine this or write down your words for them in your journal. Explain something to them that they might not understand just yet about their experience. Offer them affection and tell them how loved they are. Let them know what to expect as time goes on.

Deeper Reflection

After this meditation, reflect on how you spoke to your inner child, the way you comforted them, and what surprised you about their energy. Write down one to three ways you'll continue to compassionately parent yourself today. Write and reflect about how this may serve you in your partnerships and relationships moving forward.

PAGE of CUPS.

In My Emotions | Page of Cups

I dream, Child, that you get a second chance
In a kinder, softer world.

Character Traits: Dreamer, Imaginative, Sensitive, Unrefined, Artistic, Exploratory, Experiential, Pleasant, Sincere

Meaning

Akin to hearing the faint whisper of a spiritual awakening, the Page of Cups represents the most sensitive and empathetic inner child. The pages demonstrate areas of our personality we are getting comfortable expressing, becoming curious about, and learning from, and this page learns through the art of intuition. Often expressed through daydreaming, fantasy, and art, this character in the deck has an innocence and sweetness that can be seen as naive, but this openness is an absolute gift, a wisdom, in fact. When this card shows up in a reading, I know to validate the feelings of someone (and perhaps their wounded inner child) as they long to be loved, appreciated, and seen for their quiet demeanor and natural ability to respond to others and life through their empathy.

Page energy is similar to ace energy in tarot. This card shows that there could be an opportunity to create, embody, and express our intuition and greatest desires with joy and play. Maybe, through embracing this sensitive figure, the magic of the Universe can more freely flow toward us, and life can be led through fantasy rather than limitation.

Channel the Page of Cups

Daydream. Find a space that brings you peace, preferably in nature, and allow your mind to wander and daydream. You may remember from the beginning of this chapter that I had my water "epiphany" in the shower, during daydream and unattached observation of thought. This page has such an affinity for seeing the fantasy and dreamlike space in our everyday world that you could gain a profound appreciation by embracing an artist's mind and seeing beauty in all its forms.

Deeper Reflection

Write a list:

- In what areas and spaces do I tend to become more sensitive?
- It's OK for me to respond that way because . . .

After writing, repeat to yourself: "You are feeling, and you can share your feelings safely. You are feeling, and you can show your feelings to others. You are growing, so things will continue to change. Your body, mind, and heart are all growing. You are accepted. You are wrapped in love, light, and acceptance. You are unique. You are worthy. You are safe to be you."

KNIGHT of CUPS.

In My Emotions | Knight of Cups

I shielded myself in an armor of self-love,
became a warrior of my own worthiness.
Just long enough for you to come to my rescue.
Just in time for you not to have to.

Character Traits: Romantic, Vulnerable soul, Kind, Patron of the arts, Good conversationalist, Beautiful

Meaning

This card approaches us with tenderness. A gesture of love and romance, it's certainly a court card that most readers enjoy seeing in a love and relationship reading, and I value the way this card takes action based on feeling. The knights often represent how, where, and at which speed we are meant to move toward a goal or commitment. This knight does so with flamboyance, style, grace, and ease. Whether you feel connected to your inner romantic or feel awkward or uncomfortable leading so vulnerably with the heart, this court card is asking you to see the beauty within yourself and dare to share it with another. Or perhaps it's noting an area of your life that's driven by your heart, or a person that's approaching you with a lovey-dovey gentleness and intention. No matter the context, continue to move and respond to love and kindness.

Channel the Knight of Cups

I always tell clients to "romanticize your life" when this card pops up. Become the main character of your story and comfort yourself! Light the candle in your space, buy yourself the flowers, turn on sexy music as you cook dinner, and sway your hips. Whether you're in connection with a partner and choosing to lean into romance together, or you're solo, this powerful expression and appreciation of beauty will transfer to all areas of your life. It will remind you that without enjoyment, amusement, and those little butterflies in the stomach occasionally, what's the point?

Deeper Reflection

In your journal, recall a memory where you made choices based on love. Then reflect on the following prompt: "When I led with loving intention, I experienced . . ."

QUEEN of CUPS.

In My Emotions | Queen of Cups

There, at the very crown of her head, was a
*   huge channel of light*
That extended toward the sky and effortlessly
*   connected her to Source,*
Quite psychic herself.

Character Traits: Feminine, Intuitive, Empathic, Maternal, Generous, Healer, Creative, Soft, Appreciative, Graceful

Meaning

When this mother archetype shows up in a reading, I respect and admire her immense connection to the divine feminine and natural healing presence. A maternal court rank (queen) combined with the most feminine element of water creates a supercharged and super emotional third eye connection. This queen is intuitive with a capital I and the epitome of grace and elegance. This queen shares her wisdom and healing power through the art of connection, unconditional love, and of course psychic wisdom. Because she is a complete empath, she must consider her emotions as she often carries and nurtures the emotions of any other soul she encounters. She's quick to absorb and carry feelings and vibrations that aren't necessarily hers to hold. Healing comes effortlessly to her, so we'll often see her channeled through healing modalities, spiritual leadership, and caregiving. When she arrives, perhaps our spiritual and intuitive connection are awakened or strengthened, or we're meeting a spiritual mentor that draws us toward our most sensitive and sacred nature.

Channel the Queen of Cups

Test and validate your intuition. Ask Spirit for a sign (any sign!) that can serve as a wink of confirmation. Quiet yourself enough to hear what this sign will be. Maybe you close your eyes and trust the first clue that appears in the darkness of your stillness. Common signs we can ask for are animals, specific flowers, or anything meaningful but unique to you. This sign serves as an agreed-upon language between you and your spirit team.

As you tap in, what sign will you trust? What sign will you honor? The Queen of Cups understands that there is cocreation and communication between her and the divine. She is attuned to the subtle magic that flows naturally and is confident enough to ask for what she needs.

Deeper Reflection

As a mystic, this mother of water has a natural attunement to the subconscious mind and an ability to heal and find intuitive clarity in all realms, including her dreams. Each morning, jot down the details of your dreams. Trust yourself and your inner knowing enough to tie some of the pieces together, creating what you can only intuit as some psychic message or healing information.

KING of CUPS.

In My Emotions | King of Cups

I know I have grown because now,
When I begin to sense what's broken in
    someone,
The once-broken parts of me don't want to
    rescue them.
I don't feel an urge to stick around or provide
    solace through the cleanup.

I no longer risk cutting myself on the shards,
But I offer to help them find the broom.

Character Traits: Mature, Family-focused, Sage, Open, Responsibly healed, Provider, Trusting, Trustworthy, Wise, Stable, Masculine, Comforting

Meaning

This king kindly parents his court and sets an example for emotional maturity. Soft yet steady, his presence never overpowers or drowns out the energies of others. Instead, he quietly surrounds and connects with each relationship in his life, providing everyone he encounters with the space to feel at ease, natural, and loved. A charitable man and hospitable figure, he might come across as shy or soft-spoken, but his grace is unmatched. The King of Cups values connection, and the most admirable part of his demeanor is that he can hold both empathy and generosity and protection and boundaries in equal parts in his heart.

When he sits before you in a reading, know that you're using healthy tools to thrive in your relationships. This card is a fantastic one to pull about a romantic interest, as it shows an earnest and wise understanding of the work it takes to commit and grow with another. This king mirrors the established self-love you have worked to discover within. Outside of partnership associations, this card could also draw you toward exploring or realizing your gifts in the arts or healing practices, as the King of Cups is a natural-born space holder and creative visionary.

Channel the King of Cups

Spend some time gazing into the eyes of someone you love. Choose a partner (or yourself in the mirror) and sit across from one another. Find their eyes and look deeply into them. What do you find, feel, see, and experience when resting in their intentional gaze? Remain in silence for as long as it's comfortable (try the length of a song) to create a container of love and vulnerability for the two of you in this moment.

Deeper Reflection

Ask yourself how emotionally regulated and balanced you've felt lately. Define it as a number between one and ten, with one being the least regulated and highly unbalanced and ten being incredibly balanced and secure.

Write that number at the top of your journal page, then spend some quiet and honest time journaling. Write about the ways you could continue to hold space for your wide array of human emotions, how you'll create more balance, and how you'll recommit to (or stay aligned with) emotional peace. Write them like promises to yourself, like vows spoken to and from a mature and healthy partner.

9

In My Voice

THE SUIT OF SWORDS

The Suit of Swords, associated with the air element, asks us to get brutally honest with ourselves. It instructs us to give undivided attention to the way we communicate with others, our knowledge and learning, and our mindset and self-talk. My tip to remember what part of our experience this suit governs is simple: "The Swords rule everything above the shoulders." So associate the Swords with the areas of your body that house the words you speak, the thoughts you have, and the clarity and consciousness of your mind (your neck, mouth, and head). Thoughts and words. Simple, right?

In theory.

I think we all know that maintaining conscious communication with others—not to mention navigating the incessant mental chatter with ourselves—can be anything but easy. Just like when we don't hold enough space for each thought we have, when we read cards too quickly, their messages can feel like a jumbled mess. When we don't allow time for proper interpretation and reflection, we can feel disconnected. Our minds can become our greatest enemies, or they can be our best allies.

The Swords are easily the most feared suit in the deck. This is because they tend to be quite accurate, pointing directly at something and speaking on it with a completely transparent and no-nonsense tone. These cards do not know how to sugarcoat a message, and as such they're the ones that keep some readers from following the call to pick up a deck at all. The Swords are ready for battle, with messages that ring so true they're almost impossible to run from once we channel them. They expand and promote our growth through their precision, so it's important to remind yourself that the tough love you receive from this suit is meant to point out the areas where you have more available to heal. The characters in these cards use their weapons not to destroy, but to clear away the debris and distractions that limit our potential or keep us stuck.

While the truth hurts, it also sets us free. I realized quickly in my healing process that the more I spoke honestly about the pain I had experienced in life, the more my wounds scabbed over in a way that didn't feel so *itchy*. As I challenged myself to be more vulnerable and open about it, I felt like I had gotten my power back. Rather than feeling irritable and hindered by anxiety, for example, I would authentically share what frustrated me, and suddenly the weight of it didn't feel so burdensome anymore. This is how words and storytelling became the basis of the work I share, and it's what pulled me toward tarot in the first place; there's something so raw about the deck in general and the Swords' transparency in particular.

I have two distinct memories where I used my voice through my writing and felt profoundly different after speaking my truth. The first was when I was a senior in high school and cut class more than I honored my assignments. The exception to my deviance was English class, which I actually considered worth my time. In class, I wrote a poem about all the houses I had lived in. The writing detailed the spaces my mother and I had occupied and the themes of each. I wrote about how these houses served us in some ways and pained us in others. I wrote about how and where I felt at home and how hard it was to find comfort in a physical location when you felt disconnected from yourself. My teacher, Mrs. Smart (yes, that's really her name), read the piece and told me, "This is the best thing you've ever written, and I hope you know it was powerful." I felt proud just for writing it, but her praise made me feel even better about sharing that part of myself.

Less than two years later, when I was nineteen years old, I sat in a rocking chair holding a bundle of double-spaced papers I had printed at my university's library. I had walked the pages and my fragile body to treatment that morning at an intensive outpatient program for eating disorders and recovery. Every day we'd gather, and each week one member of the group would share details about their life. That week it was my turn. The pages housed my life story so far. The exercise was encouraged by our therapists as a cathartic activity. They promised we'd feel better if we allowed ourselves to be seen, heard, and appreciated for all we'd already tackled. They hoped our words would show us that we were stronger than the eating disorders that weakened our spirits.

I had worked on my story for weeks in my dorm room and enjoyed every minute of the writing and release. Most people in the group would share two or three pages and give a general timeline and overview of their life. They'd tell us about the sports they played in school, their sibling dynamics, their past partners, and their misaligned career paths. But quickly I had a stack of at least ten pages of stories, memories, and metaphors. I'm not sure if I had a lot to say or if the speaking and sharing just felt freeing. I wanted to let all my words fall from my mouth so badly so I could love myself enough to fill the same mouth with food again.

When I read the final sentence of my biography aloud to the group, I looked around the room. My gaze was met with eyes that felt soft and appreciative, warm and strong. I felt like others truly understood me and saw me in my experience. They related themselves, and they valued my vulnerability. Again, I felt proud of myself for writing it at all.

Today, I use tarot to encourage the same radical transparency and unedited conversations. When I'm sitting across from someone, with the cards strewn out between us, I want us to acknowledge hard things, or the "shadow" as we affectionately call these wounds in the spiritual community. I want to learn about what someone hates just as much as what they love. I want to encourage cuss words and slightly inappropriate jokes (we don't have to take ourselves or these readings so seriously, after all).

All seventy-eight cards hold a power that mimics our own, so even when the sharpest ones, like the Swords, flip over, I see them as an invitation to retell the rawest story that you've told so far. These are the truths that could rattle us yet inspire others. They shake us to our core but also carry us back home.

As you learn more about the Swords cards in this chapter, consider your inner voice. Reflect on the quality and clarity of the words you use, the tone of your vocal instrument, and how often you make music, share stories, or listen to your unique and sacred voice with care and attention. Nobody can express your story as authentically as you, so let's hear it through these cards with no apologies.

Suit of Swords Associations

Element: Air

Chakras: Throat and heart

Timing and speed: One week

Astrological signs: Gemini, Libra, Aquarius

Season: Fall

The Suit of Swords is . . .

Knowledgeable, Truthful, Adaptable, Logical, Quick-witted, Swift, Communicative, Social, Detail-oriented, Inquisitive, Blunt or direct in tone

When Reading for Yourself

It might be hard to hear some of the messages the Swords send you. This suit doesn't mean to scare you (although some disheartened readers might disagree). These truths were coming anyway, and the air element wants to wake you up to the realities of yourself even sooner so you can shine a bright and investigative light on your healing process. Their intention is to come to our rescue, although they often do so harshly. The Swords won't deliver soft poetry; they tell you straight up what isn't working in your life, even if you try to deny it.

Over the course of my personal tarot journey, as well as in my experience reading for others, I've noticed that Swords cut through a reading in divine timing. It's worth sitting in the discomfort of these themes. It might be jarring and painful at first, but eventually it can feel quite freeing to break through the limiting or rigid mindset that can start to hold us captive. I've found that sometimes the Swords present us with messages that try to come in through different cards. But maybe you weren't ready to hear it. Like an urgent alarm, Spirit finally sends the intuitive hit through this less forgiving air element. It's time for you to listen.

When Reading for Someone Else

Drop into deeper conversation. If you're pulling many Swords for someone during a reading, commit to dropping the surface-level small talk and bring more transparency to the discussion. The Swords are urging you to stop sugarcoating the story that the cards are intuitively guiding you through. Your honest and unfiltered words could be just the confirmation and clarity the recipient needs to hear.

To mimic the direct language of this section of the deck, get right to the point! Keep communication and messages from these cards clear and concise. Ground the flighty energy of the air element with some actionable directions to follow, or an affirmation to carry moving forward. Give your reading recipient an honest and memorable message to serve as their final takeaway.

Tarot Outside of the Deck

In life and in your tarot practice, stay curious. Keep asking questions and become a student of the world. You always have the freedom to change direction or pursue new interests in your life, but the air element reminds us that time and space can be fleeting, so the time to explore is *now*. Be adaptable and allow yourself to go wherever the next gust of wind or conversation with a stranger is meant to take you.

This suit has an insatiable thirst for knowledge. The tone of these cards is quick and witty. Stimulate and fuel the Swords' gift of gab by consciously changing your perspectives, having challenging conversations, and always continuing to learn.

Exercise

I've discovered that practicing active listening is really the same thing as "holding space." Believe me, there are a lot of bad listeners out there, but active listening does take skill! To be an active listener is to get comfortable with a little bit of awkward silence and instead hold energetic space for any emotions to be present along with the words. It requires us to not have a reaction, response, or immediate fix to a problem. More often than not, people just want to be heard and seen. As adults we can often pick up on what we feel we're expected to say or ask next in response to someone, like asking the "right" questions on a first date, for example. Leave behind those social niceties in tarot readings and focus most on listening and being present *before* solving. Instead of going into autopilot in a reading, following your learned script of what each card means, consider the spirit of the Swords and their directness. Listen deeply first, and prepare to tell the whole truth and nothing but the truth. Then you can facilitate a truly helpful tarot reading that supports the asker.

In My Voice | Ace of Swords

Those tiny chills,
Those dappled goosebumps
That appear when our bodies come alive,
*   electrically,*
Are like Spirit's way of sending absolute
*   confirmation.*

Keywords: Truth, Fresh mindset, New idea, Revived and direct communication, Learning something new

Meaning

The Ace of Swords is the tarot's equivalent of a "lightbulb moment." It offers a jolt or wave of absolute confirmation that sparks us to act on an idea or follow a new path for ourselves that feels honest and specific. It can serve as a sign that you've cleared some mental space and let some worries go, and now your brain can explore a new energy, perhaps something progressive, pragmatic, and functional.

The Ace of Swords is a card I love to see when someone is seeking very direct confirmation or certainty around a choice. I love shuffling and having this card swoop in to help resolve problems. If the Ace of Swords is popping up, trust your communication skills and be proud of how well you're articulating your vision with others. You're likely being conscious and deliberate in your conversations. This energy helps us speak clearly, effectively, and authentically. If you feel your thoughts are getting lost in translation, slow down and trust that you will find the right words to make an impact.

This ace is also a warm welcome when we're expecting news. Maybe you're about to receive a long-awaited email in your inbox or get a text from a special someone. Be clear and sincere in your communication. Stay open to new mindsets and perspectives.

Connect to the Ace of Swords

Opening yourself up as a channel for Spirit is less complicated than you may think. When tapping into intuitive work and psychic practices, setting an intention is really the most important step of the process. If your mindset feels muddy, your thoughts are jumbled, or your brain has a few too many tabs open, here is a powerful yet simple practice to mentally reset. It's useful before reading tarot, of course, but it's just as effective before you begin your creative work, an important conversation, or a presentation.

To try it . . .

Come to a seated position with your spine tall and the top of your head reaching toward the sky. Relax your body so your jaw releases, your shoulders drop, and your hips and legs feel heavy beneath you.

Close your eyes and envision a ball of light dancing above the crown of your head. Notice the detail of it: the color, the shape, the size. Next, state your intention to yourself and send it to the ball of light floating above you. One word is plenty, like "ease," "clarity," "presence," or "cleansing."

When you feel ready, let the ball of light drop in through the crown of your head and make its way slowly through your third eye, your throat space (pay special attention here), the center of your heart, your core, and your hips.

Fill each nook and cranny of your body with your intention. Imagine a laser beam, representing your intuitive connection, traveling through you from the crown of your head to the base of your feet. You are one clear, open, and receptive channel. Your logic is strong, but your intuition is stronger. Let this new state of openness be the space you read tarot from.

Deeper Reflection

Practice brevity in your journaling and tarot practice. Since this ace-through-ten cycle emphasizes communication, it's worth experimenting with the idea that *less is more*. Long-winded and flowery journal entries can certainly be healing, but it might be worth trying to keep your responses brief to see what comes up if you give yourself a time limit. For instance, you could try journaling for the length of one song, and then shut your notebook after.

Same goes for your tarot card pulls. Challenge yourself to pull one (yes, *only one*) card when you work with your tarot deck for the next few readings, especially if your mind has been chatty and you're struggling to quiet your thoughts. It can feel natural to clarify your cards with more cards, building on the reading with many messages and themes, but this has the potential to muddy things. Limiting your reading to just one card might bring a revived perspective.

In My Voice | Two of Swords

In one fist, I hold my feelings.
Clenched in the other, I hold facts.
I punch rapidly but can't seem to strike.
Opening my fingers,
I stare into empty hands.
What exactly am I searching for?
What clarity do I even need?

Keywords: Indecision, Uncertainty, Stalemate, Mental blocks, Lack of direction, Lack of purpose, Feeling stuck, Fork in the road, Opposition

Meaning

In this card, two sleek and sharp swords cross the center of a heart. Disrupting the flow between emotion and logic, this card symbolizes those moments where we just aren't sure what's best for us. Indecision creeps in, leaving us paralyzed. It can feel as if the connection between the head and the heart has gone offline. While it's normal to worry, feel stuck, or find yourself at a crossroads, it's still uncomfortable. When this card shows up in a reading, it could be worth pausing and connecting to the body, the breath, and the emotion behind this "freeze" reaction. If your mind feels torn, is it really in your best interest to rely on it right now?

When the Two of Swords shows up in a reading involving another person, the relationship might feel stale or rigid. It might indicate that you're at odds regarding a decision. Give one another some grace, space, and time. Forcing a decision or reconciliation will only cause more strain when this energy is present.

Connect to the Two of Swords

Practice and get comfortable with identifying two truths. Over the years, I've discussed the idea that there are two truths to everything with many clients. Two things can absolutely be true at the same time: we can be joyful *and* distressed simultaneously. We can be "totally done" with something *and* not willing to let go. We can be right and have a conversation with someone who is equally right, even though our feelings differ. Next time you pull this card, take some time to consider where you're being contradictory or, after observing the discrepancies in your life, notice where you're living two truths.

Deeper Reflection

Try writing in a stream of consciousness. This practice truly changed my life, and I can only hope that the prompts and practices across the pages of this book spark a magical, free-flowing connection between you and Spirit.

- Set an intention. Silently state to yourself (and Spirit) what you hope to gain from the channeled writing experience.

- Take time to ease the body and breath. When accessing a flow state, we must drop into the physical body and parasympathetic nervous system to fully surrender.

- Set a timer or turn on a song as your timekeeper. The beginning is the hardest part, so committing to writing for only a short set of time is a great way to start this practice!

- Write, and don't stop. If I'm struggling to find words, I keep my pen moving, perhaps repeating the same word "then, then, then, then . . ." until I find the next one.

- Let your handwriting be imperfect and loose. Once you access a stream of consciousness or channeled writing state, your hand will start flying to keep up with the creative and cathartic flow, trust me.

- Let the thoughts and feelings come through disjointed and messy. You can always put the pieces of your written puzzle back together when you're reading your writing later.

In My Voice | Three of Swords

My voice quivers from inside my throat, stuck
  yet searing with disdain for you.
It was a shock I could not have prepared for.
No words, only feelings.

"How dare you?" I ask silently in disbelief.
My lips rest, remaining closed.
My nerves race, reacting at rapid speed.
My eyes somehow glaze over,
Calm and fixated on a version of you I never
  expected to meet.

By exposing your truth, you did all the talking
here.

Keywords: Heartbreak, Betrayal, Traumatic experience or memory, Difficult ending, Hurtful experience you don't see coming

Meaning

It's hard to write about this card. As an empath, my entire body recoils in response to the sadness surrounding it. It reminds me of my first heartbreak, the one that woke me up to the truth of the world, the way others can hurt and betray us. The Three of Swords energy changes us deeply. It reflects the pain ingrained in our most hurtful memories. It creates a cellular remembrance, a reference point for what pain can feel and look like.

If we recall the numerology chapter, threes in tarot bring an energy of others to our journey. In the Swords suit, the three can signify that, unfortunately, pain has been inflicted by another. When another party speaks or shares a painful truth with us, it can feel like a dagger piercing our heart, just like the image traditionally depicted on this card. Over time, I've also learned that the Three of Swords frequently pops up to reference a trauma response, meaning the actual betrayal might not be happening in real time, but the body is responding as if it is. Our reactions are strong, our nervous systems can be triggered or on high alert, and raw emotions may definitely overrule logic when this card pierces through a reading. So when I pull it for someone, I like to ask them (or the cards) if this feeling is an open and recent wound or an old scar that's been exposed in a new way.

Connect to the Three of Swords

Try this heart-cleansing exercise:

1. Inhale and extend both arms out to create a T-shape,
    sending energy through each fingertip. As raw and
    vulnerable as it might feel, radiate your heart up and
    outward, extending your energy proudly, even if it is
    uncomfortable to feel this exposed.

2. As you exhale, bend your elbows and draw your fingertips toward the center of your chest, eventually letting them kiss your skin and tap your body.

3. Inhale again and extend your arms back out wide, inviting in fresh energy.

4. Keep repeating this, tapping between each extension and eventually closing your eyes.

As you move this way, opening and closing yourself, let any distrustful or resentful energy clear away. Make the movement your medicine. Release any lingering pain from your heart and pull it away from you so you can freely receive new love.

Deeper Reflection

Just like my channeled piece of writing for this card, begin a journal entry with the following: "How dare you . . ."

Intuitively follow what comes up and notice who you decide to write to when you confront betrayal.

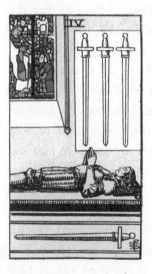

In My Voice | Four of Swords

Breathe.
To limit your breath,
To limit your rest,
Is to limit your life.

Bow in gratitude to who you are becoming,
Know that the steps to get there might not
        include steps at all.

The path can be discovered in presence
And breath
And nothing more.

Keywords: Rest, Meditation, Contemplation, Self-care, Solitude, Settling into peace despite threats, fears, or responsibilities, A pause

Meaning

The Four of Swords is the deep breath we need after the jarring and confrontational Three of Swords. When you pull this card, know that it is urging you to rest. *Please, please listen to it.* It's time to find a quiet space and seek solitude. It's time to stop overexerting yourself and realize that without a relaxed mindset, we are simply living in a state of fight, flight, or freeze. This card gives you the opportunity to choose yourself. Will you take self-care a step further than your typical routine and really use rest and rejuvenation to keep your mind sharp and your mental health strong?

A quick tip from a tarot-reading perspective: when pulling cards in the Swords suit, it's important to notice if the weapons in the imagery are facing you (threatening), within your hand (defensive), or more passive and grounded. The Rider-Waite-Smith's Four of Swords card depicts three swords looming above the figure as they rest peacefully, their hands settled into a prayer position. This is a reference to the three threatening swords they faced in prior experiences (the Three of Swords), but this time, they have a fourth sword laid beneath them. It's available as a weapon if and when they're ready to return to battle.

Life brings pain and trouble. We respond, we react, and we must defend ourselves from time to time. But we can't do anything without the energy and the willpower to keep fighting. Sometimes the most fulfilling thing we can do is take a long nap, settle into a season of deep renewal, and focus our attention on meditation and prayer to keep our faith as strong and sharp as our sword.

Connect to the Four of Swords

Practice meditation. Whatever your mindfulness practice looks like, prioritize it. There are many methods of meditation, so I won't tell you how you should practice or what approach to use. If you don't already have a meditation practice, you might try beginning with a form that feels easy, accessible, and personal to you. It would be advantageous to choose this practice sooner rather than later, as this is another way of choosing yourself. And consider starting it right away, making time this morning, tonight before bed, or, even better, right in this moment.

Deeper Reflection
Journal using the following prompts:

- The last time I allowed myself to truly rest was . . .
- Rest is my birthright because . . .
- My Spirit Guides and intuition are asking for rest when they . . .

In My Voice | Five of Swords

Maybe in another lifetime,
Power and control and competition won't be
* our chosen shields.*
Maybe we'll meet with swords down and a
* desire for peace between us.*
We can support and stand by one another in
* union,*
Rather than across from one another in
* division.*

Keywords: Conflict and competition, Manipulation, Self-sabotage, Ego, Toxic behavior

Meaning
This card is the glaring and obvious reality that all of us, at one point or another, suck. We can be competitive and combative, egotistical, and flat-out mean. This card wants nothing more than to win, even if it requires reactions and responses that are not kind or moral. Are you

losing a battle at the mercy of someone's egoic sword? Some of the ugliest tactics and most low-vibe habits are formed in the throes of this card. If it's showing up in a reading, consider surrendering. It might be best to separate yourself from this toxic and aggressive behavior, whether it's bullying, gaslighting, or even abuse.

There are more conscious ways to communicate, and the Five of Swords presents a conflict that requires you to find those healthier tactics. This card is a challenging one because (like all the tarot cards) it can illuminate something in us we don't want to look at. Is it pointing out your own self-sabotaging behaviors? Consider this before you point fingers at others.

Connect to the Five of Swords

Before every reading and whenever I leave my home, I bubble and protect my energy using my clairvoyant, or "clear seeing," abilities. It takes a little imagination and willingness to visualize and use this skill, but it's definitely doable with practice.

To try it, close your eyes and settle your energy. Picture yourself seated or standing wherever you are and imagine a mirror image of yourself in front of you. Wrap the twin version of you in a boundary of protection and light. This could appear in a number of ways (after all, there's no right or wrong with psychic visual practices). It might look like a translucent bubble or a vibrant ring of golden light circling your body to create a firm energetic boundary. I personally place beautiful white roses at the edge of my energy field or aura. I picture them floating and creating a respectful, protective barrier between my precious energy and the intensity of the world.

Find your own variation and visual representation of energetic protection, then watch it envelop you and take care of you through a supportive boundary. If or when your day feels threatening, close your eyes for a moment and reimagine it there while taking a full inhale and exhale.

Deeper Reflection

Write and genuinely accept yourself no matter what these prompts may bring up . . .

- I notice myself getting competitive in these areas of life . . .

- Beyond the desire to win, there's a deeper reason why I might fight or feel this way. I'm afraid to let my guard down because . . .

In My Voice | Six of Swords

Let yourself be carried to the shores
of safety now.
You've done all you can.
You've done enough.

Keywords: Transition, Movement, Change, Vulnerability, Reluctantly leaving something behind, Putting healing and safety first, A rite of passage, A connection with new environments, Receiving help

Meaning

This card asks us to move forward even before we're fully prepared to let go. The Six of Swords depicts a man rowing a woman and child away from turbulent waters and closer to a shore of peace.

There are multiple cards in the deck that hint and nudge us toward making a decision to walk away from something that does not serve us, but it's important to note that the Six of Swords holds a bit of reluctance or hesitation, which is why having outside support (in this case the man rowing the boat) to aid in the transition is helpful.

The Six of Swords is a card where we admit defeat and choose something healthier for our souls. It's a rite of passage; we learn to follow something truthful and freeing rather than what our ego tells us we have the willpower to muscle through. When this card arrives, we may witness an unhealthy relationship disintegrate or begin to shift our perspective in some way.

It's a card we can choose to read negatively, harping on what we're leaving behind. But we also have the option to focus on the new environments that await us when we're more open-minded. No matter what your initial feelings are around this transition, the cards are communicating that you must change, accept help from others, and release old wounds so you can evolve.

Connect to the Six of Swords

Practice setting boundaries. As the idea of "quiet quitting" and social media detoxes become more commonplace, and as millennials and members of Gen Z flock to therapy without an ounce of shame (finally healing on behalf of generations!), the conversation of boundaries has become a hot and familiar topic. When this card shows up in a reading, take an assessment of your boundaries and tighten up any that need to be honored even *more*.

These boundaries could certainly be exercised in a relationship, but if your relationships feel strong right now, consider the habits, routines, or even types of media you're consuming and engaging in. Find new ways to place and maintain boundaries that positively contribute to your mental health and overall mindset.

Deeper Reflection

Recall an experience, a relationship, or a workplace you let remain in your life past its point of purpose or comfort. Think back on a time you compromised your needs more than you needed to. Respond to this prompt: "I stayed because . . . and I forgive myself for staying so long."

In My Voice | Seven of Swords

We can trick ourselves into anything.

We hide truths like a parking ticket shoved
under a pile of junk mail
Or the "forgotten" messy leftovers waiting in
the back of the fridge.

We make it obvious when we don't want to
look at something.
We make self-deprecating jokes and find
a slew of excuses,
Sneaky mechanisms
To keep avoiding the healing
we actually deserve.

Keywords: Deceit and dishonesty, Insincere or inauthentic
in tone, Making excuses, Façades, Rationalizing false
feelings, Theft or robbery, Running away from the truth

Meaning

Before we panic about the nuances of this card, let's address the obvious: something is a little *off*. There's a strange and subtle energy, a whispered warning, nagging at you. Maybe you're concerned that someone is lying to you. This card is associated with dishonesty and distrust, so this certainly could be the case. While I sincerely hope not, as your self-proclaimed "tarot bestie" and ally in this journey to learning each card, I'm here to challenge you to look inward first. More often than not, this card references a situation that has more to do with *you* than anyone else (I know it's hard to hear that). It's time to ask yourself how and if you are being inauthentic or dishonest with yourself, others, your words, or your actions. What feels like a lie lately?

This card was incredibly challenging when I first started reading tarot. I was hesitant to talk to clients about this sneaky and secretive theme.

It continues to be one of the most uncomfortable lessons in the deck for new readers. Be gentle with yourself when reading this card, but equally challenge yourself to get to the root of whatever feels superficial, like a façade, to you right now.

Connect to the Seven of Swords
Make a confession through mirror work. (Make sure you find some space and privacy for this practice because mirror work is quite vulnerable.)

1. Stand before a mirror and hold eye contact with yourself.

2. Now comes the hard part. Speak to yourself and make some radically honest confessions. Speak your fears. Say what's making you resentful lately. Say whatever you'd like, just say it. The space is yours, and your throat chakra is ready to release.

If you *really* want to take this practice up a notch, you could always bare your skin and try this naked (hey, I have, and it really is beautiful). But ease yourself in slowly. These could be the most authentic words you've spoken to yourself in a long time. Speaking up and being heard by others can and will always be transformational, but this practice is intentionally designed to be a sacred time between you and *you*. I hope you recognize it can be just as powerful as sharing your story publicly.

Deeper Reflection
In your journal, channel to this prompt: "This is something I need to say out loud . . ."

When you're finished writing, read it aloud to yourself. Elevate your voice so it's loud, certain, and proud as you listen to the brave words you put on the page.

In My Voice | Eight of Swords

A mentor once asked me what the energy
within my heart felt like.
She asked me to feel it first, observe it without
judgment,
Then describe it in detail.
And I actually found words that fit.

"It feels like sour milk," was my strange but
honest answer.
That was the first time I truly understood that
our energy
Can lay dormant, sit stagnant, and become
rotten.
That it can accumulate if we ignore it,
Becoming less and less nourishing over time,
Taking shape into something unhealthy.
We can let anything spoil:
Our thoughts,
Our relationships,
Our feelings.
We can watch anything spoil, yes.
And equally we can let anything go when it stops feeling right.

Keywords: Feeling restricted or stuck, Imprisoned by your own thoughts, Isolation, Limiting beliefs, Victim mentality, Stagnancy, Overwhelm, Helplessness, Powerless to our own thoughts

Meaning

I have a theory that this is the most commonly drawn card in the deck. Our thoughts have the power to dictate our experience and the trajectory of our lives, and the Eight of Swords is every bit of proof of that. From the moment we are born, we are flooded with information—words, phrases, projections, and definitions of who we are, who we're meant to be, and who we never will be. Others try to condition us to fit into their world all the time, and it's exhausting.

Although we grow up in a noisy world that can be stifling rather than supportive of our dreams or desires, we can learn to dial down the volume, numb out, or close ourselves off. We decide (not because we're weak, but because we're tired) to just believe what we are told about ourselves rather than self-define or challenge the truths we never wanted to identify with in the first place.

The examples are devastatingly endless. A middle schooler who is told they're lazy by a harsh teacher might go on to believe they can never initiate a passion project because they don't have *it* in them. A woman is swallowed by judgments of her body from a toxic partner, then spends years untethering herself from the belief she's not beautiful enough. Our thoughts are our own, but they have also been influenced by the outside world.

The Eight of Swords is an energy that speaks to these limiting beliefs and engrained self-definitions. It's also a card that can make us feel trapped, isolated, and stuck in our experience. You've spoken yourself into a reality you don't want to be in, and you now feel powerless. As grim and frustrating as this card sounds, I want to assure you there is nothing but hope.

It's in this phase of the Swords cycle where we have the opportunity to master our mindset. The presence of the Eight of Swords offers a chance to begin reversing thought patterns, state more honest and loving affirmations, and move your self-talk in the opposite direction to rewire your mind. You have a chance to drown your inner critic's words and free yourself from the wrath of your limiting beliefs once and for all. How will you silence the words that tell you you're not enough? How could you take a mindful step toward freedom and expansion today?

Connect to the Eight of Swords

Try an anxiety-reducing technique called progressive muscle relaxation. This somatic practice will draw you closer to your physical form while releasing stress.

Begin at the top of your head or the base of your feet, scanning your body to locate the places that feel tense or uncomfortable. Focus on a body part and muscle group, then intentionally tense it up. For example, you could focus on your shoulders then shrug them close to your ears. Hold this pressure tightly for about ten to fifteen seconds, bringing as much tension and compression to the area of your body as possible. Then slowly release, watching your body relax, expand, and become more gracious.

While practicing the progressive muscle relaxation, repeat the following mantras to yourself:

- I am imperfect, but divinely so. I love and trust myself despite (name insecurities/flaws).

- I am free, never trapped.

- I can let go now. I am letting go now.

- In this surrender, I find my true self.

Repeat this for two or three more areas of your physical body.

Deeper Reflection
Write and reflect, connecting and speaking to your future self:
"Dear Future Self, Today, I'm setting us free. There are false beliefs that once defined us, but moving forward we will . . ."

In My Voice | Nine of Swords

They sent a frightening storm,
The kind that shook and rattled the
*   windowpanes.*
It was just strong enough to wake me up to
*   the storm*
Existing inside of me.

Keywords: Anxiety, Obsessive worry, Restlessness and troubled sleep, Poor mental health, Fear, Intrusive thoughts

Meaning

This card's energy reminds me of a boiling teapot. Shrill and alarming, it's a sound you wish to silence as quickly as you can. The Nine of Swords feels like our nightmares and fears are following us, creating a headspace that is quite the opposite of *chill*.

The air element has been accumulating since the Ace of Swords, growing anxious in energy and reaching a point that not even meditative spa music can ease. As someone who struggled with panic attacks, intrusive thoughts, and insomnia as a result of my traumas, I can empathize with how disruptive and tiring anxiety can be.

Tarot readers must become mindful, respectful, and aware of the mental health of whoever you're reading for (including yourself) if the Nine of Swords pops up. It's not a card to ignore or sweep under the rug. When anxiety, depression, fear, and trauma reach a boiling point, the best way to heal is to get to the root of it.

Connect to the Nine of Swords

This card can feel very disempowering, making us feel like victims of our anxiety or like we're at the mercy of our racing, worrisome thoughts. It's time to move some of this frenetic energy out of the body, using the voice to activate the warrior within us. You can do this by practicing throat activation:

1. Begin by taking a deep breath in to provide for yourself and replenish your spirit.

2. On the exhale, let the jaw drop and the mouth release an audible breath out.

3. Repeat this again, over and over, growing louder on each exhale. What could begin as a soft sigh should grow in volume, eventually becoming a groan or moan and finally a cathartic shout. Release the judgment of what the noises sound like because it's just noise. It's just energy moving through you to create space for more peace, quiet, and mental wellbeing.

Think of this exercise like shouting into a pillow during a childish tantrum. Throat activation and intentional release using the voice can lead us to the point of breakthrough. By getting primal and loud, we can temporarily match the energy of our fears and take our power back.

Deeper Reflection

"Morning Pages" is a practice I picked up years ago and continue to use in my daily ritual. It is the practice of free writing or stream-of-consciousness writing to pour your thoughts onto paper, preferably first thing in the morning (Julia Cameron describes this in detail in her book *The Artist's Way*). As a somewhat naturally anxious person, the moment my alarm sounds each morning, I can very easily rush into thoughts and nerves about my day. It's in that early morning light that I have a chance to either react to my worries or quiet those concerns.

Morning Pages feel very similar to channeled writing in that they're just a flow of words. There is no destination for your sentences; you're simply releasing every thought as it comes up. I typically write one to two pages; however, Julia Cameron advises her readers to write a full three pages. The writing you release can be fragmented and random. It might even read like a laundry list of things to do and people to consider that day. But at least you will have freed your mind of the "junk" you woke up with and let it become more external. You're not erasing or hiding the responsibilities or pressures per se, but you are creating a new home for all the thoughts, fears, and worries. As soon as you're done, shut your journal and move on to a loving practice. This could be breathwork, prayer, or pulling a card or two from your tarot deck. After releasing so much in your Morning Pages, you might feel lighter and more receptive to whatever the rest of the day brings.

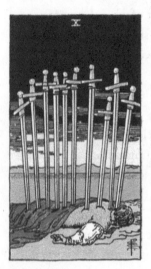

In My Voice | Ten of Swords

I've learned that if I don't surrender, the light doesn't appear.
I prolong dawn.

Keywords: Failure, Collapse or ruin, Betrayal or backstabbing, Devastating ending leading to a new opportunity, Exhaustion, Reaching a dead end, Deep wounds

Meaning

It's over, my friend.

Before I continue, I want to hold space for the fact that the sentence above could feel like the greatest gut punch right now. When this unwelcomed lesson appears in your reading, you could feel a wide range of intense emotions, from devastation to relief. Before I offer you an opportunity to reframe this ending, sit with the discomfort of this card for a breath or two. Then commit to moving forward.

When I'm describing this energy to clients or tarot students, I call it our "permission slip" to allow what's done to be done. We have likely been overthinking with all this air element circling the mind. Maybe we are even obsessing as we hold tight to something that released us long ago. Read this card as sensitively as you read the Nine of Swords because often there are toxic and abusive patterns here, too. As dissatisfying as it is to maybe feel like you failed, you must forgive yourself through Ten of Swords chapters. The time you spend worrying only holds your mental space hostage, leaving it distracted and less open to new and productive energies. It's worth eliminating worry now before beginning a new cycle.

Connect to the Ten of Swords

Put down your tarot deck and let it rest. When I start to pull the Ten of Swords consistently, I know I could be overdoing it. It seems to pop up when I'm relentlessly seeking, searching, and reiterating my desires or needs to my tarot decks and Spirit Guides rather than truly listening to the information that has already been presented. It's a card that makes us ruminate and obsess over our tarot practice, and it's a fast way to establish a distrustful relationship with your intuition. Slow yourself down and take a much-deserved break to quiet your mind before pulling cards again.

Deeper Reflection

In your journal, write with the intention of releasing. Use the following prompt to determine what finally must go: "Enough already! I've had enough of . . ."

PAGE of SWORDS.

In My Voice | Page of Swords

To my inner child:

You're a miracle
With a voice that sounds muffled right now.

But believe me when I say
The pain will stop,
Your vision will clear,
And they will

h a n g
onto
and
celebrate

The words you speak and share someday.

Character Traits: Quick-witted, Clever, Chatty, Young, Curious, Intelligent, Verbose, Talkative, Prone to gossip, Storyteller

Meaning

Far from timid or shy, this page has a bubbly energy that encourages us to get investigative about our lives and search for knowledge that will strengthen our awareness and perspective. They remind me of a child who keeps asking "But why?" over and over because no answers to their questions will ever be adequate. They believe there must always be more to learn or understand.

Because the page cards show us a side to ourselves that we could lean into more as adults, its arrival in a reading might feel like a sign to question things, reach out to others, and connect more through words and ideas. This page expresses themself best through conversation with others. They enjoy learning about why others hold differing opinions. Occasionally, the Page of Swords card can imply we're being gossipy or nosy, so be mindful of how kind or necessary some of your conversations and judgments are. Overall, this childlike figure does a fantastic job of inserting themselves into environments, conversations, and spaces that could use their wit and charm.

Get social when you pull this card for yourself! It might hint at upcoming and exciting news that's on its way (the aces and pages hold similar newness and opportunity) or tease that a conversation is about to happen at the exact right place and time.

Channel the Page of Swords

Drive your next conversation by asking more questions. If you're the friend in the group chat who shares every detail of your day, maybe redirect the energy a bit and instead ask others some questions. The Page of Swords thrives in deep conversation and finds a lot of inspiration from the words and perspectives of others in their lives. Everyone's voice and story is another opportunity to soak in new information and become wiser.

Deeper Reflection

Appreciate the element of air and the way it makes our lives full of ever-changing movement. First reflect and write: "X feels 'up in the air' in my life right now because . . . and this is why it excites me."

KNIGHT of SWORDS.

In My Voice | Knight of Swords

I can't wait.
I can't wait.
There is a feeling of anticipation brewing, and
 I'm not sure what I'm expecting.
Yet I flow with it
Because I just can't wait.

Character Traits: Swift, Responsive, Reactive, Focused, Mentally aware, Ambitious and action-oriented, Fast-thinking, Problem solver, Pragmatic and logical, Self-assured, Intense, Perceived as aggressive

Meaning

This knight charges toward us with absolute certainty and excitement, so prepare to act *now*. He's a character in the deck that can stir anxiety in the reader because he moves so swiftly and unapologetically. We can almost feel like we're under attack. Although he has an intense demeanor, I appreciate the way this knight keeps his blinders on, removes any external distractions from his mission, and moves toward his goal. I think all of us would benefit from silencing the noise of others' expectations and focusing solely on what we want, perhaps choosing to be selfish from time to time, and the Knight of Swords inspires us to follow his lead. Consider if you're charging ahead with pure intentions and strength or muscling through something just to prove yourself and your abilities. This knight is ambitious and relentless in his pursuits. Can you reflect his tenacity and fierceness? Are you ready to tackle your goals or your healing with this much urgency?

Channel the Knight of Swords

Get your heart beating, move your body, and, dare I say it, do a bit of cardio. As someone who has struggled with her disordered eating and exercise habits, please know I'm not saying this with *any* icky diet culture undertones. There's absolutely nothing you need to "burn," nor is there a reason to push or overextend your body, but the natural energy of this card is similar to a sprint, so why not mimic it through physical exercise? You could channel the Knight of Swords by completing a round of jumping jacks or going for a brisk walk or run outside. The knights are the movers and shakers of the tarot, and this character in particular is so swift and diligent in his movement that a heart-thumping cardio burst might be the jolt to the nervous system your body needs to initiate a project and move forward just like him.

Deeper Reflection

With an energy this fast and furious, it's important to consider what tools, practices, and resources you have to handle the demands. Write and reflect: "When life speeds up, I sustain my energy by doing X. I rely on Y tools to keep me going."

In My Voice | Queen of Swords

She's here to bring peace,
A mediator of the heart and mind,
Always seeking truth within herself,
So she can set an example,
Mirroring clarity
Within others.

Character Traits: Reasonable, Articulate, Observant, Honest, Misunderstood, Justice-seeking

Meaning

When this queen archetype points her sword toward you in a reading, she's drawing attention to your mindset and asking you to get clear about and proud of your authentic self. She is the ultimate BS detector. Incredibly observant (and occasionally hypercritical), this mother nurtures through tough love. I deeply respect her desire for justice and fairness, as the whole Swords family longs for a world created through honesty and truth. I admire her fantastic boundary-setting skills, too. She certainly believes that truth can set us free, but her approach to discovering and exposing these truths is not for the faint of heart. The Queen of Swords asks hard questions and isn't afraid to call you out.

This queen is ruled by the most direct and stern element of air, making her personality complex and often misunderstood. Considered the most cutthroat of the four queens, her personality is strong-willed and unapologetic. Let her inspire you to find your own voice of reason and cut to the chase in your healing experience. It might feel raw, but know there is a well of unrelenting love at your fingertips.

Channel the Queen of Swords

Take up space by claiming some more of it. It could be time to assert yourself more in conversation. Maybe there's an opportunity to take a risk by throwing your name in the hat and applying for a position you're not perfectly qualified for, or sliding into the DMs of a cutie you have your eye on. We often worry about being *too* direct, *too* forward, *too* off-putting. Forget that BS. Especially as a woman, I know I can worry about inserting myself or filling too much space. Once you pull this card, spend the rest of the day finding ways to claim more, fill each room you walk into with more of your authenticity, and share yourself unapologetically.

Deeper Reflection

Rather than writing, nurture yourself with your own silent retreat. You can Google and find the fancy retreats offered for thousands of dollars where you're forced into silence in a stunning five-star experience—and that honestly sounds like a dream—but you can also exercise the discipline to do it yourself.

There are very accessible ways to create a "silent retreat" experience right in your own routine. This could look like deleting social media apps and silencing your phone, then taking an oath of silence for a period of time. By embracing less chatter, you're opening the opportunity for more inner dialogue. For a length of time that feels realistic, refrain from consuming media, podcasts, and even music. Try holding only the words of your inner thoughts and see where that silent conversation takes you and how comfortable you are in it.

KING of SWORDS.

In My Voice | King of Swords

I whisper,
Not because I can't be loud,
Because I've been loud for too long.

Character Traits: Cerebral, Confident, Wise, Uncompromising, Intellectual, Perfectionist, Fair, Invested in truth, Rational, Values systems, Teacher, Leader, Trustworthy

Meaning

When this king confronts us in a reading, he stares at us directly from the center of the card. His position mimics his authority and certainty, and we can sense he holds a message for us. He pushes us toward greater intellectual depth, mirroring our wisdom and ability to use discernment. The King of Swords is incredibly decisive, with impeccable judgment of character and opportunity, so chances are he's showing up to let you know a decision and choice is on the horizon, one that you likely already know the answer to. While he's more stern than soft, his apparent calm, cool, and collected personality invites us to embrace a similar demeanor and confidence in how we lead, speak, and connect.

This card is a great one to see in a reading if you're looking for something (or someone) serious and forthcoming with their intentions and vision.

The King of Swords is a thoughtful leader of a team, director of a group, or delegator, so consider if you have the same skills and if this card is urging you to take on such a role.

Channel the King of Swords

Be decisive and willing to have the final say. For one whole day, speak up and be the decision-maker and thoughtful leader in your communities and groups.

I'm not asking you to steamroll conversations or ignore other people's preferences, but try to notice when there's indecision in a team meeting or when you and your partner are doing that familiar dance of "I don't know, what do *you* want for dinner?" Take the guesswork out and make a decision thoughtfully and confidently.

The King of Swords can execute his vision with incredible tact because he doesn't second-guess himself. When you pull this card, don't be afraid to step up and make choices for yourself and those you care for.

Deeper Reflection

In your journal, consider the following: "These are the personal values, ethics, and morals I'm proud to carry with me . . ."

10

In My Purpose

THE SUIT OF WANDS

The Suit of Wands, associated with the fire element, asks us to live purposefully. Notice I said *live* purposefully rather than "find your purpose." Longing for a purpose or specific reason for your existence is honorable in theory, but it can be painfully difficult in execution. I can't count the number of clients who have asked me for direction and support in finding their purpose during a reading. They long to understand the impact they could make or ways they could inspire others if only they just knew *how*.

The Wands serve as a creative compass, helping us take one small (but meaningful) step at a time. The fire element is charged up in such a way that it can send little clues to draw us closer to what we're meant to be doing, challenging us to move toward what piques our curiosity and naturally captivates our attention.

Much like immediate sexual chemistry with a partner or ideas that come to you in the middle of the night, some things can't be forced. My tarot practice and relationship with the cards have taught me this time and time again. Instead of searching fruitlessly or labeling ourselves as lost, I believe we can shift our focus and embrace the "next right thing" approach. This is when we take the opportunity to drop in with ourselves at any moment, feel into our deepest knowing, and ask ourselves, *What should I do next?* This pause gives us a chance to tap into our intuition and clarify what feels satisfying to us in the here and now. Becoming comfortable with our self-reliance and our instincts help us build confidence. When we practice making empowered decisions and following the beat of our own internal drum, we soften the expectation that each reaction and choice must lead us somewhere profound or needs to mean something more. Some decisions are the correct ones based on the way they make us *feel*.

I have a distinct memory of walking through New York City with a work friend. Steps from Union Square Park, we were wandering into boutiques, killing time before an event we were hosting together, one sponsored by a kombucha brand with a popular social media nutritionist speaking on gut health.

I had cofounded a wellness event planning business, and I was enjoying the work, but I wasn't *loving* it. I was proud to be an entrepreneur and pleased with the way we had built a health-conscious community, but as a highly sensitive person, I often felt drained by the amount of energy and mind-numbing attention to detail that was required to host events. Nonetheless, I was present in my business; I assumed this would be my path for quite a while.

I mention my lack of questioning during this chapter of my life because I find it important. Today, I realize my professional open-mindedness and nonattachment to any idea of soul purpose was the exact laissez-faire attitude I needed to wander not only into a store with tarot decks but effortlessly toward my future passion and purpose.

My friend and I perused a store full of home goods and furnishings. I wasn't in the market for anything new for my apartment, mostly because I was in my early twenties and broke. But I noticed a striking black box that said "TAROT" on the bottom shelf of a small display in the center of the store. Maybe it caught my attention because it looked out of place among a bunch of decor, or maybe a bit of luck just called me to it, but either way, I reached for it.

I had never held a tarot deck before, but I instantly knew I really wanted that one in particular. I didn't know I'd use this deck for years to come and eventually place it in a sacred space in my (now better furnished) home, retiring it after years of client sessions. I had no idea how many times we'd work together, or how the box would eventually look so tattered and worn, or how the cards' edges would become soft and frayed.

"Are you ready to head out?" my friend asked as she interrupted this fateful meeting with my gift.

"Yeah, but I'm just going to buy this quickly." I couldn't articulate why, but purchasing this deck truly felt like the next right thing for me to do. If I hadn't, who knows when I would have experienced the healing power of the cards or learned new parts of myself through their lessons?

Later that night after the event, I opened the deck in our hotel room and thumbed through the guidebook and each of the stiff new cards. I loved some of them immediately, but I was terrified of others. Today I realize how natural these aversions are and how normal it is to fall in love with some cards at first sight. I pulled my first couple cards and questioned everything about what I was doing and receiving. But boy, it felt good to experience this guidance.

So that was the beginning of my tarot practice. I easily moved from novice to invested learner to practitioner to professional over the years. Parallel to my personal interest, my purpose was evolving unknowingly but simultaneously each time I reached for my deck and asked for their messages. While some of my spiritual rituals and stress-reducing routines were harder for me to keep up with, tarot was always quite natural. I had to set reminders on my phone to meditate daily and schedule my therapy at the same time each week so I wouldn't forget to show up for myself, but tarot made its way into my days without any effort, no matter how busy my life felt.

I can confidently say that I have never missed a single day of my tarot practice since I purchased that deck in New York close to a decade ago.

While my collection of decks has grown and many of my conversations with them are now centered around the healing of others, these cards live and breathe beside me.

Tarot led me to do more valuable inner work and self-reflection. It retold me my own story with love and inspired me to share it in new ways, and it became my favorite pastime and area to study and eventually teach. The tarot seamlessly built a new, much more aligned business with me, nudging me gently out of what was no longer serving me and toward something that would feel more impactful and true. And to think, if I wasn't wandering or wasting time in NYC one afternoon, my purpose might have been delayed!

I try to remember this when I'm stuck at a fork in the road, feeling uncertain or unclear. I tap back in and remember these moments where I led myself through instinct rather than logic. What feels like the next right thing for you?

Suit of Wands Associations

Element: Fire

Chakra: Solar plexus

Timing and speed: One to three days

Astrological signs: Aries, Leo, Sagittarius

Season: Spring

The Suit of Wands is . . .

Transformational, Powerful, Passionate, Destructive, Creative, Ego-driven, Masculine, Inspired, Determined, Strong

When Reading for Yourself

Develop a healthier relationship with your ego.

You are gifted. You, reading this book, playing with tarot cards right now, are full of unique talents that nobody can express as beautifully as you can. Don't you recognize your strengths?

Ego is such an interesting and often frowned-upon topic in spiritual communities. In some spaces and conversations, it comes across as an area of our soul experience we should shun, silence, or be ashamed to express.

My take? We are experiencing this lifetime as human beings. We can own that! We all have an ego, and it is part of our healing to develop a healthy relationship with it so it can become the engine moving us toward our most fulfilling life.

When you're learning about the Wands cards, don't be afraid to express *your* healthy ego and personal identity. Your energy is unlike anyone else's, so enjoy and embrace your natural gifts, healthy relationship with your worth, and limitless potential as you experience the practices and prompts offered here.

When Reading for Someone Else

Hype it up! The more fire element I see across a reading, the more encouraging, empowering, and coach-like my role looks. I become a personal cheerleader, and the most fascinating thing is that this tone appears almost automatically, without me thinking about it too much. That's how strong and magnificent the Wand's suit and fire element energy is. It stirs and lights something up within us, so when these cards are present in a reading, I'll often talk about the power we each hold and the way we are so unique and radiant, just like fire.

When you're reading these messages for another person, don't be afraid to confidently declare that they are meaningful and special. They carry divine magic in their aura, their essence, and every corner of their soul. You're part reader, part motivational speaker when the fire element and Wands suit light up a reading!

Tip: Spice up your readings! Get creative and develop new reading styles. Ask the cards different questions or try seemingly unconventional approaches to pulling, shuffling, or using your cards. The Wands suit offers us a chance to destroy the conventional and prioritize playfulness and adventure. This is a great opportunity to get more innovative as a tarot reader and find your "flavor" as an intuitive and channeler.

Tarot Outside of the Deck

In life and in your tarot practice, follow what *fires you up*. Your creative outlets and natural pull toward certain activities say a lot about what your soul craves. I encourage you to become invested in these interests. Don't stifle them; lean in! In my healing journey, my fascination was centered around tarot. It lit me up and inspired me in ways that other spiritual modalities didn't hold a candle to (see what I did there?). I certainly hope you find this practice as inspiring as I did when you pick up your cards.

And while this book is focused on your independent journey and inner healing initiatives, I also challenge you to become an advocate for more than yourself. Allow the fiery Suit of Wands energy to guide you toward the causes and social justice movements you deeply believe in. Use your voice to confidently speak up for what matters most to you and express your perspectives to keep the dialogue moving toward transformation and change. The fire element isn't afraid to dismantle or destroy the old, so consider how you can spark necessary change in your communities.

Exercise

Take on the YOLO (I know, my millennial is showing) mentality and remind yourself that life is short and precious. It's worth being ridiculous and not giving a damn what others think of you. Whether that means you wear what you want to wear (to hell if it's trending on TikTok), move your body wildly at the next concert, sing loudly with your windows open, or eat cake for breakfast, stop playing by the rules all the time. The fire element doesn't want us to be boring. Our experience as human beings is quite complicated and difficult enough. It's up to you to give yourself moments that feel out of the ordinary, transformative, and magical!

ACE of WANDS.

In My Purpose | Ace of Wands

Once you've had a taste of work that leaves
  you both
Full and insatiably hungry
At the same time,
Once you've found "it,"
Money and power don't satisfy;
The soul takes a different currency.

Keywords: A spark that inspires a creative and passionate new cycle, Initiation, Chemistry, Immediate attraction, Artistic genius

Meaning

When the Ace of Wands flashes from my deck, I know the energy is about to feel more organic and exciting. It initiates inspired action. Whether that's the bold and unplanned first move toward someone of interest (ooh la la!) or the genius idea we receive randomly in the shower, it ignites a fire in our belly. This flame is magnetic, pulsing, and promising. The opportunity in front of us could be a strong *hell yes*—that is, if we're prepared for the passion, authenticity, and confidence that will be required of us for execution. This ace can feel quite random and, often, fleeting. If we aren't careful, it can disappear like a small match being blown out by a gentle gust of wind. We must tend to the Ace of Wands by creating a protective and stabilizing environment (i.e., having the lifestyle, tools, and completed self-work to keep our egos in check on this journey). Allow your wildest dreams and passions to draw you in. Stay authentic and humble. You are a gifted and unique source of light, and this ace invites you to discover why.

Connect to the Ace of Wands

Sit in the morning light. Fantastic for setting our circadian rhythm and balancing our hormones, waking with the sun and spending around fifteen minutes in direct sunlight in the morning can help reset and nourish the body and spirit. Each morning presents an opportunity to approach your day with the same freshness and enthusiasm as an ace, so try prioritizing vitamin D and see the impacts of integrating this warm solar energy into your spiritual experience.

Deeper Reflection

Write a list of everything that inspires you, spikes your curiosity, or elevates your interest. What do you feel excited about day to day? Then write a list of everything that makes you feel purposeful and important.

Read both lists and see where there are similarities and connections. How are your natural passions similar and complementary to the confident actions you boldly take?

In My Purpose | Two of Wands

The belly takes a deep breath, growing and
    shrinking
Over and over, expanding and contracting.
In the same way my confidence varies,
Meek and quiet in some spaces and intense
    and proud in others.
I deserve to fill all the rooms,
Claim all of my space,
And occupy this earth.
Like my breath, I've discovered only a fraction
    of my fullness.

Keywords: Bold vision, New direction, Brave choice, Wild possibilities, Planning, Craving something more

Meaning

The Two of Wands gives us a sneak peek into our potential. It's a courageous card because it leads us to vulnerable self-inquiry, prompting us to consider what will truly fulfill us.

In the card, a figure stands at the top of a castle, dressed lavishly with a globe resting in the palm of his hand. Looking out past the allure of the world in front of him, he appears dissatisfied with this already familiar environment. Maybe, like them, your current path is keeping your thirst quenched, but is it *enough*?

You may pull this card and have an itch or desire to change something. What might happen if you tried something new and took a chance on yourself? You might be on the precipice of a big decision, and the butterflies in your stomach are probably responding right now, jittery and unsure.

I lovingly call this card the "five-year plan." It doesn't reference some spontaneous risk we must take; it's a slower build toward a promising future via thoughtful planning and vision holding.

There's no denying that something lit a fire under us with the Ace of Wands. Now we have a curiosity we can't ignore. Whether you choose to believe you're divinely guided by something greater or you're just open to learning as you go, this card nudges you toward a fated destiny that you have the independence, will, and ability to seek out and discover.

Connect to the Two of Wands

Practice Breath of Fire, or Kapalabhati Pranayama. This breathwork technique is highly energizing, detoxifying, and warming, just like the element of fire. It generates physical heat to inspire movement of energy. Like revving an engine, this practice can spark initiation from within you. When we are looking for an answer, this type of connection to our confidence and healthy ego is crucial before we make a monumental leap or power move. In the yoga community, this practice is called "ego eradicator," as it has the power to break down barriers and walls that limit our potential and inhibit our alignment.

Common in the Kundalini style of yoga, this breathwork is highly active, so you'll want to start slowly and build stamina over time.

1. Sit with a tall spine in an upright posture and rest your hands on your belly.

2. Take a deep, cleansing breath in through your nose and exhale out your mouth to prepare.

3. Inhale deeply again, this time filling your belly about three-quarters full of air. In a quick motion, forcefully exhale all the air from your lungs as you snap your navel toward your spine. Let this movement stem from your diaphragm.

4. Allow your lungs to fill up again naturally, snapping back to refill with little effort, then contract the belly and breathe again.

5. Do this about twenty or thirty times, then allow your breathing to go back to normal and observe any feelings, like buzzing or humming, in your body.

Deeper Reflection

Consider the following prompt: "If I knew I wasn't leaving anything or anyone behind, I would do X, and I would explore Y."

In My Purpose | Three of Wands

Forgive yourself for the time you spent fearing your power
Or choosing paths you shouldn't have traveled.

Trust that these subconscious interventions and detours
Were your soul's way of knowing best
And preparing you.

Keywords: Confidence, Clarity, Progress toward goals, Freedom, Personal success, Risk paying off, Happiness from choices made, Optimism, Future planning, Moving or traveling

Meaning

Gaze down at your feet and take a look at where you've landed because chances are you're proud of where you stand. Having made the choice to pursue something in the Two of Wands, the world now feels more hopeful and bright in the Three of Wands energy. There's new terrain to explore and freedom at your fingertips when you connect with this card. This optimism is shown in the Rider-Waite-Smith tarot deck through an abundance of the color yellow, which is considered an optimistic color in the tarot. The figure is no longer surrounded by the mundane, gray, cold atmosphere of their previous environment; finally they're enveloped in cheerfulness and light.

Tarot readers often ask me to give them more detail about this card. At its core, the Three of Wands is simple: you have chosen yourself and prioritized your desires, and you should keep following your own lead. Trust that the journey will continue to unfold as long as you stay dedicated to yourself.

While the Three of Wands is not necessarily a complicated or challenging card, it is authentic, and I'd say that's a pretty fantastic way to be living, healing, and showing up for yourself.

Connect to the Three of Wands

Visualize your ideal life. Creativity is encouraged! An ideal life visualization is an opportunity to witness your higher self's greatest life and desires through an imaginative, sensory experience. As a professional psychic, I've been met with the question "What's in my future?" before. Whenever someone asks me to predict specifics for them, I try to focus on the *feeling* they are calling in and the circumstances that will support their highest good and soul alignment. I try to immediately deviate the conversation from fortune telling, and instead channel something more empowered, so it feels like the client and I can cocreate this ideal together.

To try it . . .

1. When you feel settled and safe to tune inward, close your eyes and relax your body. Become as present and still as you can.

2. Ask your future/higher self to show you a vision of you in the future experiencing your soul's ideal day. Wait a moment and allow the scene to develop naturally; don't force anything!

3. Using your psychic sense of clairvoyance (clear seeing), watch, experience, and notice what's ahead for you. Observe your future self and where you are, what you're wearing, what toys or tools are around you, and if there are others nearby. Do you recognize anything that's currently in your life?

4. Take as much time as you'd like here, moving about your day and imagining your dream life in detail.

Deeper Reflection
Write and reflect:

- What risks have I taken lately?

- In what ways am I proud of myself?

- Where am I noticing my uniqueness and inner light?

- How can I stay committed to sharing my light when my confidence wavers or my external world tells me to dim it?

In My Purpose | Four of Wands

Wide-eyed, we look at each other
With mirrored amusement
And silent acknowledgement,
An unspoken sense of "We did it. We made it.
*   We're here."*

We rest in bewilderment,
Marveling at the complexity,
The audacity,
The miracle,
That love and life could bring us to this place
*   at all.*

Keywords: Celebrations and joyful experiences, Shared memories, Prosperity, Reaching milestones, Engagements, Weddings, Major announcements, Achievement

Meaning

The Four of Wands is a homecoming. It's a celebration, a party, or an initiation into an exciting next phase. I always make the joke that if you're at an event where you serve a cake, you're probably in the midst of a Four of Wands moment. Naturally, engagements, promotions, graduations, weddings, and other loving and joyful occasions fall into this card's energy. The Four of Wands offers an experience that we want to share with other people because we want those we love to celebrate with us, too.

The four wands stand upright in the foreground of the card, ushering you beyond the threshold toward a more evolved you. There are fantastic manifestation opportunities here. The vibes are great, and our love for life is leading us. This card is the reminder that happiness and joy can magnify and call in more happiness and joy.

Because it's a four in the tarot numerology cycle, it presents exciting yet stable energy. We are always making moves and taking steps toward the future, but when the Four of Wands pops up when I'm reading for someone else, I know they deserve to relish in the moment because they have done enough for now. It's important to become present and fully appreciate this special time.

You're doing an amazing job, I promise you. Take this opportunity to dance and honor all the parts of yourself you've healed so far.

Connect to the Four of Wands

Dance! You can dance with a partner or by yourself, but please dance. These instructions may feel cliché and expected for a card about parties and celebrations, but our reasons to dance are sometimes few and far between. When you pull the Four of Wands, create a party in the present. Sometimes the easiest way to activate a higher vibration is to turn on music and move your body in a way that expresses your commitment to your inner work. Use your physicality to access your birthright: joy.

Deeper Reflection

In your notebook, creatively express yourself for one full song. First, pick a song you absolutely love. Maybe choose one that reminds you of a particular Four of Wands celebratory memory or special chapter in your life. Then start doodling. Intuitive drawing is just like channeled writing: there are no rules; it's just creative space.

Maybe set the intention to draw what your joyful heart looks like and express it through shapes, lines, and symbols. Pour yourself into your pen and onto the page while savoring the lyrics and melodies of the song you chose to be your soundtrack.

In My Purpose | Five of Wands

We're hesitant to express anger,
And I never understood why.
When you start to suppress it,
Think of a roaring thunderstorm.
Even our mother needs to kick and scream
    sometimes.

Keywords: Chaos, Confusion, Anger, Resentment, Conflict, Challenges with others, Disagreements, Resistance, Obstacles

Meaning

This card is intense and chaotic, often without reason to be. This energy has a short fuse, so ask yourself if your temper is being poked or if your reactions are getting wild, hostile, and unpredictable. The Five of Wands usually brings up a disagreement, but the fight could burn out quickly if you take a moment to collect yourself.

In the Rider-Waite-Smith deck, this card shows five men quarreling with their wands. I lovingly mock this energy by saying it's similar to teenage boys in the yard fighting with sticks. If you looked into it, you'd probably find this brawl pretty pointless.

Ask yourself where you're responding to a situation as a fighter instead of a lover. What is your battle for? Is it even important, or have your emotions become so heightened and intense from the element of fire that you're frustrated without true reason?

If you pull this card, chill out and find a less reactive way to overcome an obstacle you might be facing. We all make mistakes, and we all say things we don't mean or react harshly from time to time. If you're getting all worked up for nothing, this card is calling you out on it. Any aggressive or extreme behavior is only keeping you away from a more productive state of mind and a more purposeful way to channel your energy.

Take an honest assessment of where all your time is being funneled as well. Are there too many responsibilities on your plate, too many cooks in the kitchen, too many opinions, too much expectation, too much tension, *just too much?*

If so, what would quiet some of this chaos before your responsibilities and expectations become things you resent? Remember that anger is often a secondary emotion to a more vulnerable part of us that feels threatened, alone, unworthy, or scared. The Five of Wands has the power to either keep us distracted or bring our awareness back to the root cause of how to honor our needs, energy, and individuality.

Connect to the Five of Wands
Stop, drop, and connect with a different element. Just like a fire that's out of control, sometimes the best thing to do is cool it down and stop feeding it more fuel. When you next pull the Five of Wands, do something to snap you out of this frantic energy and back into a more grounded physical experience. Taking a cold shower (water) or going outside and grounding yourself in nature (earth) are two great ways to get out of the emotional response and back into your body.

Deeper Reflection
In your journal, write a list of two to four things that deeply irritate you, stuff that pisses you off. These could be little annoyances from members of your family or pet peeves that irk you to no end.

After finding a few examples, write about what's possibly behind that anger. What do you *really* feel behind your frustration?

In My Purpose | Six of Wands

The fibers of each feeling I had
Wove themselves into a new fabric to warm me.
I sewed these pieces together to create something
*   extraordinary,*
And today I allow it to drape over my chest
*   and shoulders.*
It is my beautiful armor,
A victory adorned in my own self-discovery.

Keywords: Glory, Victory, Being seen and heard, Finding yourself in the spotlight, Self-confidence, Inflated ego, Public recognition, Good news, Accomplishment, Fame, Pride, Leadership

Meaning

The Six of Wands is the tarot equivalent of a victory dance. We've been waiting for this chance to show off our gifts and successes, and finally there's an audience to appreciate and marvel at us, applauding our efforts. This confident and boastful energy enjoys being in the spotlight, and if this card struts through your reading, you're probably being recognized for a job well done. Congrats! This card traditionally shows a victorious warrior on horseback traipsing back from battle through a crowd of onlookers. We can assume they just endured the fight depicted by the Five of Wands.

When you pull this card, ask yourself who might be noticing you and your efforts. What have you been doing exceptionally well? Is it time to let yourself receive even more attention for your creativity and passion?

It's a phenomenal card to pull if you're looking for a promotion, pay raise, or praise about you and your work. After taking risks earlier in this cycle and following your unique and special purpose, the Six of Wands is the reminder that we stand out to others when we stay true to ourselves. Our confidence can be felt far and wide; it's warm and alluring to others. Remember that your most authentic self has the power to inspire others, and you are worthy of being seen while in the glory of your accomplishments.

Connect to the Six of Wands

Humblebrag! Listen, if there's any card to inspire your confidence, this is the one. Subtly (or not so subtly) share your latest good news, who you are, and why you're incredible to anyone who will listen. You can rush to share with your friends, the recruiter in your LinkedIn messages, or the kind stranger willing to listen as you lay your mat next to them at yoga. It's okay to fill spaces of conversations with our achievements. Actually, it's more than okay; it's healthy!

While the Six of Wands can often take on a professional association because it's related to our successes and passions, it can represent personal wins, too. For example, I remember when I was newly engaged. I swear I was flashing my left hand around like I was constantly swatting a bee from my face, wanting someone, anyone, to notice my pretty new symbol of commitment. I loved my new label as a fiancée, sure, but I mostly wanted to feel seen in my genuine love. I was totally seeking social media likes to celebrate, and I appreciated the messages congratulating me to honor the milestone, because that celebration didn't feel like an icky brag. Those who love me knew the healing it took to prepare for partnership, and they appreciated our healthy, authentic relationship.

Your humblebrags deserve to be heard because they mirror the fight you've put in to heal and become this incredible version of yourself.

Deeper Reflection

Explore what it means to be in the spotlight. How much of what you do is fueled by a desire to be recognized? How comfortable are you really when you're seen for your gifts and skills? Begin your writing with: "To me, fame means X. If/when I achieve it, I'd honestly feel . . ."

In My Purpose | Seven of Wands

My ego shouts.
My authentic self says, "That's it?"
My ego screams.
My authentic self mocks me. "More."
My ego roars.
My authentic self says, "I'm still louder."

Keywords: Self-defense, Standing your ground, Protecting yourself, Courage, Boundaries, Perseverance, Bravery, Passion

Meaning

In simplest terms, the Seven of Wands says, "Back the [insert your preferred expletive] off." It's a protective card, and usually it's testing our commitment to our beliefs and stances.

My favorite detail in the Rider-Waite-Smith image is that the man is wearing two different shoes, implying that he didn't anticipate the fight but popped right up to rise to the occasion.

Another detail I love is the way he crosses the wand directly in front of his vulnerable heart, a barricade to block anything from dimming his personal power or the light he holds within. It's a card that I believe can swing between two clear extremes: on one hand it's fantastic to have clear boundaries and be willing to protect and go to battle for what you believe in, but on the other hand, it can hint at some defensiveness and reactivity within someone's temperament. As a reader, you get to be the judge.

This card is a seven, so numerologically speaking, it's a time for reconsideration and increased self-awareness. If you pull it, you might notice a need to protect your choices and speak up loud and proud, or maybe you're on the receiving end of some very defensive energy. You'll notice that the fire element is polarizing. It's so intense and transformational that if we're not ready to embrace it, it can manifest into a great deal of anger and ego rather than creativity or confidence. Like a wildfire, the heat builds throughout the cycle, and each numbered card in the cycle grows hotter and hotter, its energy almost frenetic and more difficult to contain than the last.

Connect to the Seven of Wands

This card feels territorial and primal. One of our most natural instincts is the need to nourish and feed our bodies. When a great deal of courage and force is required of your body, creativity, and mental energy, supplementing your inner strength with food and nutrients is key.

Consider the quality of your food and eat for the solar plexus when you pull this card. Eat hearty whole grains and plenty of plants to maintain your stamina. Some foods related to this chakra/element are yellow lentils, squash, lemon, pineapple, bananas, and complex carbohydrates like brown rice and sweet potatoes.

Deeper Reflection

In your journal, write some of your non-negotiables for living a passionate life. Clarify for yourself what your creative spark and inner warrior need to stay authentic and true to your purpose.

Make specific notes of what is *not* welcome in your aura (energy field) and life, clarifying what deters you from your path and compromises your gifts. Some examples may include office gossip, friends who don't reciprocate, or alcohol. Then write down your must-haves that keep your confidence high and give you energy.

In My Purpose | Eight of Wands

Brace yourself
For breakthroughs.

Keywords: Speed, Movement, Expansion, Travel, Freedom, Exciting news, Unexpected opportunities, Hopefulness, Anticipation, Communication and outreach

Meaning

A welcome energy in the cycle of the Wands, this fiery eight feels like a nudge from the Universe and a reminder of why it's worth following your gut. This card can bring unexpected opportunities or serendipitous encounters that lead to expedited results. It pushes us toward a more fulfilling destiny, although its energy may surprise us or feel like it's coming out of nowhere, like a wild card. I enjoy seeing this card for anyone in any situation because it brings extra light and momentum to their personal healing, relationships, or professional experience. It speeds things up!

In the Rider-Waite-Smith depiction, there are no people shown on the card. There are simply eight supercharged wands moving in sync through the air. This imagery perfectly sums up how the energy of the Eight of Wands isn't about taking specific action. Instead, it's about channeling and receiving universal energy and support. It comes to our aid when we could use some momentum or high-vibrational confirmation that we are confidently following our authentic beliefs and truest paths. It can equally intervene and take us to better paths, allowing us to continue to heal and evolve from an even more purposeful place. It's within this card that the Universe can give us the experiences and opportunities we deserve as a result of our courage.

There's also a reference to travel in this card. Whether you choose to plan a getaway, use the theme of expansion, or cultural exploration, or seek a new environment, this card promotes getting out of your comfort zone.

Connect to the Eight of Wands

Do a little self-care switcheroo. Pick a routine you practice regularly. It could be the time of day and the way you journal, the exercise class you favor, or the type of music/podcast you listen to as you work. Now, switch it up! The redirection will not only start to shake you out of a rut, but it might creatively inspire and attract new ways of thinking, channeling, and receiving.

Deeper Reflection

Recall a memory where life brought you events that were unexpected, unconventional, or random, yet aligned. Begin to write and reflect, connecting and speaking to your future self: "Today I want to redefine 'adventure' and 'the unknown.' I'd like to make them less intimidating. Let me share with you, Future Self, how beautiful it is to experience the unexpected . . ."

In My Purpose | Nine of Wands

Most days, I aim to move with grace,
Until all I have left is force . . .

Keywords: Fatigue and depletion, Persistence and perseverance, Accomplishing a goal, Resilience, Feeling wounded, Exhaustion, A test of faith

Meaning

When I pull the Nine of Wands, I picture a boxing coach encouraging their athlete in their corner of the ring. They massage their shoulders, offer water, dry their sweat, then send them back off into an independent yet passionate fight. While you're possibly bruised and certainly exhausted by the effort thus far, this card serves the same role as that encouraging coach. The Nine of Wands reminds us to never give up despite challenge. Because the card is so far along in the cycle, we know that the journey is reaching its end (it's about time!) and there will be the opportunity to celebrate after just one more brave push. Although the body could be experiencing burnout, your spirit remains strong and resilient.

If you pull this card, try to recall the Ace of Wands inspiration that initiated this path in the first place. The fire element forces us away from the mundane and toward the magical and unique path for us rather than the expected one. This requires bravery, as it is a chance to finish what you've started and muster up that last bit of momentum. This card's energy, and your response to it, will make you quite proud.

Connect to the Nine of Wands

Embrace the challenge of the card and dig deep within yourself physically to find even more strength. On a yoga mat, begin on all fours, pressing your palms into the ground and stacking the shoulders over the wrists. Stabilize yourself on your hands and knees, and when you're ready, lift your knees so you're in a high plank position (to modify, keep your knees down, but scooch them back a bit). Fire up the belly and engage your core. Take a look down between your fingertips to keep the spine elongated, and breathe.

Steady yourself and quiet the voice that tells you that you can't remain in this position. Mimic the challenge you're facing in your life with this physical representation of your body's resilience. Test yourself, holding this plank for longer than you believe you can, then repeat encouraging words to yourself as you beat the clock (and your inner critic). When you've reached your limit, drop your knees and sit back in child's pose. Rest your body and appreciate that you can do very, very hard things.

Deeper Reflection

Tune in with yourself and ask, "How burnt out do I feel today?"

Rate your burnout on a scale of one to ten. Write that number down at the top of your journal and write a full page exploring why you feel this way, if the burnout feels warranted, and if you're passionate about what is exhausting you.

In My Purpose | Ten of Wands

My guides try to lead me toward clarity.
They know I can get wrapped up in the
bitterness of what was,
So they push me toward the light of what is.

Keywords: Burden and stress, Obligations and responsibilities, Struggle, Losing focus, Heaviness, Overworking, Unnecessary worry

Meaning

Okay, I admit this will feel a tad literal, but for a moment pretend you're holding ten large logs in your arms. Ten of them. It's heavy, right? They're restricting you from heading toward your desires, and they likely feel pretty cumbersome and awkward as you juggle them against your body.

The Ten of Wands brings a similar sensation. This card represents the discomfort and stress that can come from carrying too much responsibility or holding the worries of others rather than focusing on ourselves. The fire element is unique, radiant, and captivating, just like you! When we begin to shine our inner light, follow our destined path, and confidently show up in the world, we become attractive to others—magnetic even. Like moths attracted to a flame, over the course of this cycle you've been generating more warmth and passion, and your essence can be felt by others. As you carry such a magnetism, it's almost inevitable that you attract more responsibilities and energies from others due to your gifts and power.

In some ways this card is an empath's worst nightmare. It asks us to discern what energies are *actually* ours to carry. The figure in the card is blinded by the load he is burdened with, unable to see even a few steps in front of him, and therefore needing reprieve from all the weight. As readers we can look at this card as our chance to "take a load off," unpack, and rearrange the heaviness of what we carry. We get a chance to decide what inspires us enough to keep fulfilling our responsibilities and manage it all.

Connect to the Ten of Wands

Create an environment of softness to recharge. Not only is there a lesson in boundaries here (it's definitely time to set some), but there's also a need to rebalance the exaggerated masculine energy coursing through this card. The body, mind, and spirit may be feeling incredibly tired when the Ten of Wands manifests. Before beginning a new cycle, take time to recharge and create physical space to welcome more softness.

Some ideas to create an environment that fosters more divine energy:

- Diffuse essential oils and add fresh flowers and greenery to your space.

- Play soft instrumental music throughout your home rather than any genres that feel stimulating or trigger anxiety.

- Take time away from screens and superficial light. Favor time outdoors in sunshine and use softer, ambient lighting in your home.

- Keep plenty of lush blankets, pillows, and textiles that feel cozy around your house.

- Most importantly, find some time to be truly alone in this sanctuary you create, even if it's just an hour away from your kids or an afternoon break from your computer.

Deeper Reflection

Just like you started this chapter writing a list of what inspires you in the Ace of Wands, take inventory of what ignites versus stifles your inner fire. Take a new sheet of paper from your journal and list all the daily requirements you have day to day. List where you are needed, what you are responsible for, what your expectations are, and what you do daily.

Then do a simple but effective exercise of circling the things you *must* do, underlining the areas of life that you love and enjoy doing, and crossing out some of the responsibilities that you could release, set boundaries for, delegate, or take some pressure off. To live our fullest and most vibrant life, we must recognize what's not fulfilling us or that personal power and take steps to do less of it, making more room for our unique inner fire to burn and intensify.

PAGE of WANDS.

In My Purpose | Page of Wands

What if rather than wandering through
a maze
She busted through one of the walls that
surround her
and found a path for herself?

Character Traits: Thrill-seeking, Adventurous, Rule breaker, Creative, Leader, Traveler, Artistic, Spontaneous, Brave

Meaning

There's something infectious about this page and their sense of wonder. I wouldn't label this card as wise or an "old soul" by any means. In fact, the opposite energy courses through the veins of this page, creating a hunger that drives exploration far and wide. This page is playful and excited to try any and everything, knowing that when creative energy calls, they will discover something new about themself if they follow it.

I have always made the same joke when I teach this personality to a new reader. Imagine a young Sagittarius attending their very first Burning Man. (This always gets a laugh.) This page doesn't carry much concern for what others think of them, and it's because of their charm that they not only have a fabulous time, but also attract and inspire others to appreciate their fearlessness. They choose to express themselves freely through their creative visions, urging you to do the same through travel, exploration, and pursuing new interests. They also have the ability to grow into a natural leader, evolving through the remainder of the court cards ranks (knight, queen, and eventually king). For now, though, they're enjoying the present and making life feel like an adventure.

If you pull this card, ask yourself how spirited you feel and how dynamic your experience has been lately. This childlike personality prefers to live in Technicolor and never wants to view the world as gray. Consider how and if you're beginning to dim your inner child's light, and ask yourself (and the world) the questions you need to shake yourself out of any rut you're in and get back to a vision that excites you.

Channel the Page of Wands

Fire (or candle) gaze. The sense of wonder is strong in the Page of Wands, and the elemental inspiration is palpable. Stoke your kinship with fire by gazing at the natural dance of a flame through this open-eye meditation technique. Also known as Trataka, this yogic practice stimulates concentration and settles a distracted mind.

Simply set yourself up a safe distance away from a fire or candle and gaze into it, concentrating on your breath, your focus, and your inner fire.

Deeper Reflection

Recall a memory where you were spontaneous, ignored the conventional, and took a chance on yourself. Write a letter to the version of you just before you took that risk and congratulate yourself on being brave enough to seek a new thrilling adventure.

In My Purpose | Knight of Wands

It seems like my warmth
Draws others closer
When I truly love and admire
The resource
That's heating me from within

Character Traits: Charismatic, Social, Charming, Warm, Humorous, Dedicated, Adaptable, Inspiring, Unique, Playful, Ambitious, Friendly, Visionary

Meaning

The Knight of Wands moves with haste because his quest is so important to him. He holds a bold vision for himself that is nothing short of extraordinary, and he would prefer to build a life according to his own unique terms, ditching the rulebook. The Knight of Wands breaks the boundaries and limitations of the expected by relying on his instinct, his natural abilities, and his self-assured goal setting. As a trailblazer, he's bound to make changes to the world through his work, creative talents, and leadership qualities. He understands that charm and, dare I say it, flirtation can help him win the hearts of his supporters and establish an audience of onlookers who want to cheer him on as he succeeds.

When this knight brings his fire and passion to you via this card, get excited. His energy is infectious and all-encompassing. Your greatest dreams are within reach due to your confidence and connection to personal power. This card could be asking if you're willing to keep taking risks on yourself, knowing you will eventually be recognized for how truly gifted you are.

Channel the Knight of Wands

Envision your ideal outcome. Pause and lift your gaze from the task at hand and pan further out to see the bigger picture. *Why* are you doing the work you're committed to?

The Knight of Wands has a knack for seeing the greater vision. That's why he's incredibly skilled at leading a team to victory or jump-starting a truly impactful mission or new venture. He is willing to do the work (all the knights make moves), but he also has a sense of purpose leading this effort and a committed confidence to give his wildest dreams a chance.

List your contributions to the world without minimizing the ways (small or large) you bring value to your home, family, work, and so on. What do you offer the world through the daily actions you take?

Next, take a look at what you listed, and ask yourself:

- What's the BIGGER picture work that I'm doing?

- Why am I willing to do it?

- What's the through line and commonality here?

Write freely first, then read it and come up with a mission statement for yourself. This will help you shift your focus to the horizon of where you're heading and consider the large-scale impact you have. Like a ripple effect, our energy can be sensed and felt by many more.

Deeper Reflection

In your journal, list the traits and characteristics that other people in your life compliment you on. Acknowledge and admire in yourself what others see in you, then write and reflect using the following prompt: "My talents include X, Y, Z, and this is how I use them . . ."

In My Purpose | Queen of Wands

When I worry that I've gone too far or become
 "too much" for someone,
I remember all the things that we can crave.
Gluttonously, we find comfort in sex, sugar,
 and money.
Too much or just enough becomes the question.

Maybe I do make people uncomfortable,
Maybe I'm tempting,
Maybe I'm addicting,
Maybe I'm just myself.
Either way, I've decided I'm just enough.

Character Traits: A powerhouse, Feminine, Strong, Bold, Opinionated, Protective, Multidimensional, Resilient

Meaning

This queen captivates us with her presence. Immediately we want to know what her story is and how it began. As the quintessential cool girl in the tarot, she exudes a certain energy that we admire, or perhaps even envy. We can't help it; this queen has a certain "It Factor." She's warm, genuine, and has an infectious personality that makes us feel seen, heard, and welcomed into her life and circle. A socialite, she will never shy away from the spotlight, be it through performing arts or other creative or passionate pursuits. The Queen of Wands refuses to shrink her energy. She's brave and bold enough to ask for more attention when she wants it, and she always stands firmly in her worth. She is also the first queen to rise and defend the people she cares about. This archetype has seen shadow and difficulty, and her confidence stems from a profound healing and resilience built through challenging chapters. If she mirrors you in a reading, know that you too hold this feminine power and divine strength. Your confidence is authentic, so don't hold back. Seek out opportunities to share your natural gifts and skills. Your light cannot and will not be dimmed, and your spirit will only rise from the ashes of past healing if you're connected to her energy.

Channel the Queen of Wands

Be sensual and embrace your sexuality. Sex is our natural and raw instinct; it runs through a spectrum, and it's a space to explore and question equally. Sexual expression will look unique and individual of course, but the fire element and this suit hold an intense sexually charged energy. This queen is the most embodied and unapologetic in the deck. If you've pulled her, you could be feelin' yourself and exuding a natural sex appeal and confidence, so lean into this passionately, be it through self-love or with a partner. Say goodbye to the patriarchal and stifling ideas of how we *should* express our sensuality, and write down and reclaim what makes you feel sexy in your own terms.

Deeper Reflection

Consider a time in your life when you felt like you were *too much* for someone, something, or somewhere. Decide what emotion was linked to that experience, and identify if it made you feel shame, embarrassment, or invalidation.

Hold space for the feeling by sitting with your eyes closed, your hands gently resting on the solar plexus (just above the naval). Repeat the following affirmation to yourself softly: "My light is my own, and I am just enough."

Then in your journal, continue exploring your "enoughness" and begin your writing with the following: "I am enough because . . ."

KING of WANDS

In My Purpose | King of Wands

I won't live among the shadows
Of a bunch of apologies anymore.
I will look less for the confirmation of others,
And choose to thrive in a knowingness for and
of myself.

Character Traits: Purposeful leader, Commanding, Masculine, Talented, Regal, Entrepreneurial, Magnetic, Prideful, Powerful, Unforgiving, Overbearing

Meaning

When this king parades through a reading, he carries an awe-inspiring power that can intimidate just about anyone. Confident beyond measure, his position in the court is never questioned because he's earned his title as leader and thrives in that role. This personality is an absolute visionary. He feels most himself when he can execute his vision while guiding others to follow him on his path. At his best, this king inspires others through his creativity, entrepreneurial gifts, and strong sense of self. But the King of Wands is also highly masculine, and sometimes his delivery comes across egotistical, insensitive, or like he's steamrolling others to finish first.

Easily the most natural leader among the court cards, if you pull him in a reading, your confidence and leadership is being highlighted and encouraged. Now is a time to selfishly pursue exactly what you want. Trust your abilities and go for it!

If you find this king representing someone else in your experience, consider if their warmth is helping you find your inner light or passionately distracting you from your goals and desires.

Channel the King of Wands

Consider mentoring someone who would appreciate your guidance. Once we obtain a certain level of skill, we can choose to compete and hold as much power as possible as we strive to be the best and only leader, or we can share our power with others who are still developing confidence in their craft. If this card has followed you for some time, you're strong, capable, and have much to be proud of. Consider sharing your expertise with a mentee who would feel supported and inspired by your knowledge and passion.

Deeper Reflection

The King of Wands is a "love him or hate him" type of personality. In your journal, reflect on the following statement: "I cannot be liked by everyone, and that's okay. I stay true to myself and my vision by . . ."

11

In My Story

THE MAJOR ARCANA

I've told you so many parts of my story, and now it's time you use these remaining twenty-two cards to focus on and celebrate your own. We've learned that the Major Arcana holds the greatest weight in the deck because it represents our strongest pull toward soul growth and spiritual evolution. These archetypes hold the secrets to our deepest alignment, greatest purpose, and most authentic expression of self. They're the heavy hitters and my favorite part of the tarot system. If you thought the kings and queens carried "main character energy," wait until you meet some of the spiritual teachers in this section of the deck!

The Major Arcana archetypes are like keys, each of them capable of unlocking a specific part of us. These cards soften and humble, and they remind us to follow the natural ebbs and flows of universal energy (and trust me, sometimes it's a rollercoaster through these cards). Having navigated the physical realm in the Pentacles, the emotional Cups, the logical Swords, and the passionate Wands, you're now ready to embark on a more spiritual journey alongside The Fool.

The very best thing I ever read about tarot (although I can't, for the life of me, remember the source) was this distinction between the Major and Minor Arcana: the Major Arcana holds the universal force, while the Minor Arcana tells us what to do about it.

As soon as I read this, something clicked for me. I understood instantly that I didn't have to know exactly how to respond to any of these seventy-eight cards in the deck; I just needed to acknowledge and honor what they were trying to teach me. The Major Arcana creates a theme and anchors the reading in meaning, and the Minor Arcana gives us more of an instruction manual for how to move from point A to point B.

Throughout this chapter I'll share journal prompts and affirmations rather than physical rituals or practices like in the previous chapters. Consider the spoken affirmations as grounding statements you can repeat to yourself as you navigate these different soul lessons and chapters of your life, just like The Fool. The writing prompts after each affirmation will ask you to drop into a memory or experience that aligns with each card's theme so you can notice where and how you have already witnessed examples of these complex archetypes in your life.

Reminders
Because these cards carry a slightly different tone than the cards we've previously studied, I'd like to offer some supportive reminders and tips for reading the twenty-two Major Arcana themes in this chapter.

1. The story is never truly over.
The Fool's experience is ever-changing and evolving, just like yours. While we could complete the cycle at the final card, The World, it's inevitable that a new cycle will open, redirecting us right back to the next fresh start. The tarot system is cyclical, with no truly defined beginning or end. There is a chance to repeat cycles with newfound wisdom and a deeper connection to our hearts each time. In tarot, just like life, we get second (and third, and fourth . . .) chances.

2. Patience is everything.

These cards move slowly, like, through an entire lifetime. While we're used to the quick burn of the Wands or the more rhythmic flow of the Cups, the Major Arcana requires the most patience as a new tarot reader. These are the larger life lessons that take time for us to discover or confront, not to mention understand and integrate on a soul level. These cards might feel difficult to apply and connect to your lifestyle right now, and that's okay! You, just like The Fool, are growing. Allow these lessons to sink in at just the right time, as your consciousness expands and your intuition strengthens.

3. Give the Majors weight in your readings.

While I never want a card to feel intimidating or uncomfortable to sit with, I strongly encourage you to embrace the gravity of these cards in the Major Arcana. Their meanings are complex. They push us toward taking big leaps of faith. They can become the chapters of our lives we'll look back on and remember forever. For this reason, allow each of these lessons to hold proper significance in your reading. Major Arcana cards can (in my opinion, they *must*) become the primary thread or theme that runs through your tarot spread as you receive intuitively from your reading. What I like to do is take a look at the cards I've pulled, assessing first if there are more Major Arcana cards than Minor Arcana. If there is an abundance of Major Arcana energies, I take extra time to reflect, consider, and lean into those cards in particular.

4. Notice the details.

Everything in the tarot deck was placed there intentionally. When an artist creates a deck, they mindfully choose the colors, settings, and even the direction the characters face. Everything is truly there for a reason. Really examine each Major Arcana card and find their small but significant details because these cards in particular tend to hold a great deal of symbolism, no matter what deck adaptation you're reading with. In this chapter I'll reference some symbols with each card, bits and pieces of the Rider-Waite-Smith deck that really stood out to me as I studied, but know that this is just scraping the surface. I encourage you to do continued research, looking up more of the details you may find.

5. Enjoy the journey.

While the tarot brings up themes and lessons that aren't always comfortable, I'm a firm believer that no matter what, we can keep this process fun. Enjoy this journey, especially if the tarot practice is still new to you. I always tell my tarot students that I envy them a bit. I'm jealous of the way they're meeting these cards for the first time and are experiencing their magic as they shock and delight us with accuracy and profound messages.

As someone who pulls cards daily and for a living, I can tell you that the sacredness and specialness of the practice doesn't wear off, so it's important we keep the journey of learning fun, light-hearted when appropriate, and never stagnant. These cards are like life partners to me, familiar and comfortable. My pulling practices provide a safe space for me to sit and honor myself. But I remember the beginning, when the cards still felt like strangers. Each time I reached for the deck my nerves felt like I was preparing for a highly anticipated first date. Much like the vulnerability of any new encounter, an intuitive "hit" can feel like butterflies in your belly. This joy of intuitive expression becomes your way of reclaiming the feminine and accepting the miracle of your intuitive gifts, and it serves as a chance to be unapologetic about a practice that's been shunned and stigmatized for far too long. Enjoy this journey back to yourself, friends.

In My Story | The Fool

Restless in the mind, I realize it's time
To drop into the new.
I watch an uncertain-yet-confident body do
    the hardest thing:
Leap, not knowing what or who will catch me
But myself.

Keywords: Taking risks, Leaps of faith, New beginnings, Freedom, Foolishness, Redefining oneself, Innocence, Spontaneity

Element: Air

Meaning

Numbered at zero, this is the first card in the deck and marks the true beginning of our journey. Our protagonist in the tarot, The Fool, looks and then immediately leaps with little regard for consequences, trusting that he will learn along the way. As readers, we embody this archetype every time we sit to pull cards and connect the messages with our memories and experiences.

The Fool is on a quest to discover his personal identity, divine purpose, and spiritual evolution through connection to himself and others. This card displays a character who is young and foolish, but he's also quite brave and wise because he has a willingness to trust and surrender, which we know takes great vulnerability.

Since it represents a time for new beginnings, I consider this card a chance to redefine ourselves or wipe the slate clean, no longer judging the past and instead hopping spontaneously and enthusiastically into the future. It's a fantastic card to pull if you've been calling in change, newness, and redirection. Sometimes the beginner knows better than the worried and fearful expert. Ignorance is bliss, isn't it? The Fool enjoys his journey uninfluenced by others.

There are a few visual notes and symbols that reiterate this energy. First, The Fool stands at the edge of a mountain range, and mountains represent challenges and obstacles in the tarot. Surrounded by an abundance of yellow, the skies are clear and the sun beats down on him, enveloping his energy and aura with optimism and positivity. Carrying just a small pack of belongings, he is choosing to take very little with him into this new chapter, planning to gather and find all he needs along the way. His companion, a dog, stays loyal and close to his feet, but he's also giving a warning, reminding The Fool he's courageous but not invincible.

Affirmation for The Fool

"I embrace the unknown because I learn more about myself each time I leap."

Connect to Your Story

In your journal, write about a time where you tried something new *before* you were ready.

In My Story | The Magician

Magic isn't something I search for or choose to believe;
Magic is something I live within.

Keywords: Aligned action, Manifestation, Taking initiative, Power, Skill, Focus, Influence, Willpower, Not letting anything hold you back

Element: Air

Meaning

The Magician stands before us with pride and purpose. He exudes confidence and his demeanor is powerful yet graceful.

This card represents our willingness to take our biggest dreams and grandest manifestations and make them our reality. It offers a glimpse into our potential. It's a card that encourages us to see the absolute magnificence of our existence and highlights our ability to cocreate with the Universe through our personal power, active efforts, and focus. When you pull The Magician, consider how much more you could attract and create for yourself by taking initiative.

This archetype holds a harmonious balance of all four elements: passion from fire, adaptability from air, intuition from water, and stability and reason from earth. Together, they combine to alchemize and align The Magician, supporting his gifts and skills. If you notice this card coming up in readings, take account of your natural abilities and show them off to the world!

Occasionally, I'll pick up on a "fake it 'til you make it" energy through this card. There's an air of confidence required, even though the Magician is only one small step into the soul-searching process of the Major Arcana. While there is somewhat of an inflated sense of self here, there's no denying the strength and assurance of this character in a tarot reading.

Affirmation for The Magician
"I choose to channel and align myself with the magic of life."

Connect to Your Story
In your journal, write about a time when you executed something flawlessly and with confidence.

THE HIGH PRIESTESS

In My Story | The High Priestess

At a young age, my grandmother taught me
to howl at the full moon,
The first of too few examples that being a
woman means something.

Tipping our heads back, shouting into a
megaphone held against the mouth
of our power,
A spotlight shining on us
On a stage bathed in lunar light,
We howled.

Feeling unstoppable in that moment,
I'd somehow find myself mute again by sunrise.

If I have a daughter someday,
I'll have her howl at the moon
And then wake her up each morning to growl at the sun.

Keywords: Intuitive connection, Psychic abilities, Inner
wisdom, Sensing the unseen, Waiting for answers rather than
seeking them, Mystery, Sensuality, Subconscious mind

Element: Water

Meaning

There's a sense of mystery and allure that flows through this card, and
it serves as an introduction to our own intuitive depth and higher consciousness. The High Priestess is all-knowing, a psychic through and
through. She holds spiritual information and wisdom that we could integrate into our journey should we choose to discover and access new parts
of ourselves. What I appreciate and value most about this archetype is

her ability to use subtlety and softness to speak volumes, showing us that some of the most profound energies are not obvious.

In the Rider-Waite-Smith deck, she sits in front of two pillars with abundant and decadent pomegranates behind her. Her position tempts us. Pillars in tarot hint that there is information to access beyond them, so she's alluding to the idea that we can taste the same sweet and potent connection with our higher selves if we believe in our psychic abilities. "Would you like to meet your higher self, too?" she asks with a smirk.

When she arrives in a reading, she's instructing us to speak less and listen more. Her presence suggests that we can start to tap into and express our own intuitive senses to discover greater power within. This card wants us to trust and rely on our gut instinct and third-eye vision above all else. While The Magician card taught us what we were capable of channeling and initiating change through action, The High Priestess's wisdom illuminates where we can find spaciousness, information, and connection through grace.

The High Priestess is in no rush. When you're reading this card for yourself, know that access to more information could be on the way. Waiting could serve you better than rushing to respond to the situation.

Affirmation for The High Priestess
"I trust my divine and deepest knowing. My higher self speaks through me."

Connect to Your Story
In your journal, write about a time in your life when your intuition was spot on. What led you to that clarity?

THE EMPRESS.

In My Story | The Empress

As women we are . . .

Painter and muse,
Child and mother,
All at once.

Stand in front of the mirror naked and tell me
you don't have an eye for art.
Tell me you don't believe in miracles.

Keywords: Abundance, Femininity, Fertility, The divine mother, Creatress, Living harmoniously, Experiencing good health, Art, Natural beauty, Closeness to nature

Element: Earth

Meaning

The Empress nurtures. She is the mother archetype in the Major Arcana, and she carries a deep respect for her tremendous and sacred role. She parents us as tarot readers by guiding us to notice the beauty, art, and miracles of our earthly experience and physical form. She helps us recognize how beauty speaks to us and *through* us. We are all divine creators.

This card exudes femininity and sensuality, cradling us in a divine love and appreciation for the Earth and the creative potential that's held in our wombs. The Empress understands that she can create and mimic a world *within* her that is as satisfying as the nature and environments she enjoys *around* her. This energetic embodiment is her gift, and she teaches us that we can rest in appreciation for our bodies and the naturalness of our imperfections. The Empress creates and effortlessly manifests more for herself through this gratitude. She is a woman in her divine power, and she's asking you to sit and embody your worth, too. This card can also urge us to birth something or unapologetically share something with the world that is uniquely our own.

The Empress is absolutely a pregnancy-related card, but remember that "birth" can mean so much more than creating new life. Creative endeavors, healthy and wise relationships, sacral healing, and themes of the mother wound run through this card, too. It's often a card I read as a rite of passage and expression of womanhood. It's a card I am thrilled to share with female-identifying clients who wish to amplify their love for themselves and savor the sweetness of their existence as mothers, dreamers, artists, and muses.

Traditionally The Empress is depicted seated on a throne of comforting pillows, with her body surrounded by abundant foliage to mark that she is the queen of the natural world. This card wants to know if maternal energy is moving through you, whether in the literal sense or metaphorically, and if you're enjoying and embracing that feminine energy and gift.

Affirmation for The Empress

"I am the Divine. I create and share art while in my divinity."

Connect to Your Story

In your journal, reflect on your relationship and experience with the word "mother."

THE EMPEROR.

In My Story | The Emperor

Nothing feels safer than hearing the lull
of the engine
As I drift between sleep and window-gazing
While you drive us back to our home.

Keywords: Patriarch, Stability, Authority, Structure, Foundations, Protection

Element: Fire

Meaning

The patriarch of the Major Arcana, this masculine archetype holds a great deal of authority, control, and power. While his divine feminine counterpart, The Empress, is the ruler of the natural world and organic creation, The Emperor rules over the material world and emphasizes logical structure. Because he is pragmatic and lives through rules and regulations, it's pretty common for readers to resist this energy when they begin reading cards. It can feel overly serious or stuffy, like it's projecting fatherly advice that you didn't really ask for.

When this card comes up, I recommend you pause and ask yourself if the energy is truly oppressive. The Emperor is obviously patriarchal (and therefore we might assume problematic), but his intentions are pure. I find the beauty of this card lies in how seriously he takes his responsibilities as a divine provider. He sits so assured on his throne as he defends, protects, and prioritizes his family and loved ones.

Throughout my years of reading cards, I went from seeing this card as controlling and rule-obsessed to treating it like a lesson pushing me to take ownership of my life. The Emperor is trying to share his strength with us so we can channel his leadership qualities toward what we care about as well. He helps us connect to our will so we can execute and fulfill the dreams and intentions we've tapped into through the previous cards of the Major Arcana sequence. The vagabond Fool can't grow and evolve without a little structure, so at this point in his journey (and therefore yours), it could be time to assess your systems, organization, and processes.

You'll notice that the figure in the card is dressed almost entirely in red, a color of personal power and intensity, and he carries a small golden sphere in his left hand, which represents the world he rules over and carries. In the imagery, this father literally holds a world of possibilities. You hold a power that's just as strong.

Affirmation for The Emperor

"I carry the gifts of leadership, but I use my power to protect, not intimidate."

Connect to Your Story

Write about a time when you witnessed (or channeled) divine masculine energy.

In My Story | The Hierophant

My spirituality is not above me;
it lives within me.

Keywords: Seeking knowledge, Divine wisdom, Teacher, Traditional beliefs, Ethics, Morality, Commitments, Conforming to traditional paths

Element: Earth

Meaning

The Hierophant is our spiritual teacher in the Major Arcana, and he confronts us with a presence that is traditional, all-knowing, and serious. This card is a reminder that we are on a quest for understanding and belonging in this lifetime. It emphasizes the systems, order, and constructs that our society abides by. These formal institutions include higher education, organized religions, large communities with common values, and contracts such as marriage. Because of this traditional tone, it's common to resist the energy or find it rigid rather than supportive. After moving through a spiritual awakening during the visits from The Magician and The High Priestess, followed by the personal identity focus of The Empress and Emperor, our young Fool has learned much about himself, and this card requests his attention and higher learning. It's at this point that a new lesson awaits from his next teacher, The Hierophant.

This leader's spiritual values are something he wants to pass down, and in a reading, this card can represent a mentor-student relationship. The Hierophant sits before two pillars and two followers sit or kneel in front of him, taking in his wisdom so they may learn and evolve to their own destined role. He is traditionally depicted with two keys crossed in front of him, one representing the conscious mind and the other representing the subconscious mind, two opposing but necessary parts of our experience. It's like he's challenging us to use the same tools to unlock new knowledge and information within ourselves.

The Hierophant also bestows us with new inner wisdom, like a mentor, which we learn and master through repetition and loyalty and eventually pass down when we become teachers as well. When this card arrives in a reading, I know that conventional learning and spiritual seeking are at the forefront, and we're being called to practice our spirituality "by the book." Ask yourself this difficult question: Are you becoming a follower of the crowd rather than the leader of your destined life?

Affirmation for The Hierophant

"My higher self seeks new knowledge, and I trust I'll find my teachers."

Connect to Your Story

Write about a time you followed the status quo or did what was expected of you. Did it serve you?

THE LOVERS.

In My Story | The Lovers

I've chosen before.
I've chosen based on logic and other people's
needs and what was expected of me.
Today, like a child, I'll play dumb.
I'll choose based on my heart,
Like a Fool in love.

Keywords: Love, Harmonious partnerships, Soulmates, Union, Trust, Value-based decisions, Balance, Peace

Element: Air

Meaning

This card can be summed up in one word: harmonious. The relationships that are built in the sanctuary of this card are soul-quenching, satisfying, and full of inspiration. The Lovers card represents people who will hold a special place in our story and hearts. It's at this point in the Major Arcana journey that The Fool realizes he cannot experience this cycle of life alone, nor should he. Love and genuine connection are two of our birthrights.

While the previous archetypes illuminated parts of our personal identity, this is where the energy shifts and we rely and focus on our connections instead. Relationships aligned by this card are loving ones, and we find richness, purpose, and a unified strength in them. The card absolutely points to promise and potential with romantic partnerships, but soul contracts of all kinds (including platonic) are governed by this energy as well. ·

Beyond this nod to love, The Lovers card also sheds light on our core values. In the previous card, The Hierophant, we explored society's expectations of us and how comfortable or uncomfortable we feel with those pressures. This is our opportunity to challenge relational values, asking ourselves what we find most important in our relationships based on our individual codes of ethics, then build trusting partnerships in response to them. The Lovers often appears in a reading when we are going through a chapter of making important decisions that consider our values. It's in our best interest to find people who support our ideals and want the very best for us on whatever path we choose.

In tarot, the more color and variety of color in a card, the more hopeful and destined its energy. In the Rider-Waite-Smith version, there's a rainbow of color represented as the two lovers meet in the middle, naked and exposed to one another under the watch of an angel (some believe this is the archangel Raphael). Life becomes more colorful and dimensional when others infuse their energy into our experiences, so if this card has found you, look around and notice who makes your life feel fuller.

Affirmation for The Lovers

"I sing vibrations of love. I attract others who tune into the harmony and song of my heart."

Connect to Your Story

Pen to paper, write about a moment when you fell in love with someone.

In My Story | The Chariot

It's no longer about time wasted.
There is always new time
To claim.

Keywords: Ambition, Determination, Confidence, Courage, Using willpower, Success, Victory, Masculinity, Brute strength

Element: Water

Meaning

Get ready and get set because it's really go time now! The Chariot requests our movement and immediate response. It's an ambitious energy full of determination and courage, so when you pull it, you can quickly pick up on the fact that action is ahead of you.

When The Chariot shows up in a reading, you can take it as your spiritual instruction to seek out exciting opportunities. Use your confidence to help you find new doors, opportunities, and environments to explore for yourself. The Chariot is warrior-like, so there's a bit of forcefulness and brute strength behind him as he overcomes challenges and learns his resilience throughout the process. This card teaches us that we do not have to take no for an answer.

I want you to think of this energy as resembling The Fool, but this guy upgraded his car. The speedy warrior will arrive toward his destination faster, and with less trouble, in his new chariot. The road ahead of you is still unknown, sure, but it won't be so bad because you've acquired more knowledge and more understanding of the potential for both wins and failures. His chariot is led by two sphinxes, one black and the other white, and these opposite energies represent lunar and solar forces. Far in the background of this card, there's a bustling and established city, a nod to the familiarity he's choosing to leave behind. Holding a wand just like The Magician, he uses it to channel universal energy through his body, aiding his mission to bring his manifestations and dreams to life through divine connection.

If you receive this card in a reading, consider the challenges that are currently in front of you. Ask your Spirit Guides to support you as you tap into an ambition and confidence you might not be used to showing the world.

Affirmation for The Chariot

"I set aside fear and instead rely on my vision. I can and I will."

Connect to Your Story

Consider the last time you relied on willpower and determination to get through an obstacle and write about how it challenged you.

In My Story | Strength

My first tarot deck was missing a card within
a week.
Paranoid and frustrated, I judged myself for
being so careless.

I treated the cards delicately, whispering thanks
to them each time I called on their
guidance.
How could I? How did I mess up already?

A novice at pulling cards and keeping
them orderly
But even more oblivious to the fact that
my deck
Created a plot that would write me straight toward my purpose
In such an ironic way.

I lost the Strength card
And learned through an imperfect deck of 77 cards for years,
Unknowingly tapping into a passion and strength
I didn't know I had in me.

Today I realize the card never truly left;
I just took its place.

Keywords: Inner strength, Resilience, Healing, Overcoming self-doubt, Pride, Serenity, Taming the inner critic, Softness

Element: Fire

Meaning
This card is profound. It shows a calm and steady woman wearing white (to signify her purity and kindness) as she tames and soothes an

unruly lion. Her loving gestures and attentiveness bring this fearsome creature to a state of peace, willing to receive her loving touch. She pacifies a wild animal, a metaphor for how strength can also feel soft, how healing can be gentle. The Strength card sheds light on the darker parts of ourselves and our memories and helps us learn how we can navigate the depths of our wounds with kindness rather than judgment.

What I enjoy about this archetype is that it emphasizes self-compassion. It often speaks to the times we've self-soothed and stayed steadfast, committed to our growth. The Strength card represents the battles you've fought with grace. When connecting with a strength so powerful, you should be incredibly proud of yourself. The theme here is bravery, and through our brave acts we can begin to learn about our innate gifts and greatest strengths. This card also mirrors our bravery and courage to engage in inner work, and it rewards us with the loving presence from a healer, the one we are for ourselves and carry inside our hearts.

The Strength card is a feminine counterbalance to The Chariot's brute force and action. When I'm reading this card for a client or friend, I like to mention not only how strong they are, but also how the tarot might be offering clues here about their potential to guide others in healing. There's something graceful and truly special in all our narratives. This card sometimes appears when we are on the brink of discovering a purpose within us, and now we have the power to share and give back to others so they can receive through these exquisite parts of our energy.

When this card acknowledges you in your readings, keep healing how you're healing, friend. My only advice is to shower yourself with even more appreciation. You are remarkable! You've tamed the roar of inner beasts you carry with love, and that's worth celebrating.

Affirmation for Strength
"Through grace and understanding, I can heal."

Connect to Your Story
Write about a chapter in your life when you had to be resilient and brave. How did you feel in the moment and afterward?

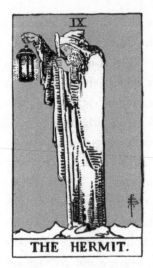

THE HERMIT.

In My Story | The Hermit

I'm hunting and gathering this season,
Finding something, be it abundance, safety, or
*   truth.*

Self-sufficiency guides me,
And I provide for myself
Because I feel most satiated by my
*   independence,*
By the resources I can gather with my bare and
*   beautiful hands.*

Keywords: Isolation, Solitude, Honoring your inner voice, Holding space, Self-discovery, Enlightenment, Introspection

Element: Earth

Meaning

The Hermit is a wise and quiet figure in the Major Arcana who relishes in his solitude. His presence feels peaceful and still. He chooses independence, even if only temporary, in an effort to reconnect with himself. During readings, this sage merely approaches us. He doesn't ask for information or conversation; he's likely just passing by. His soft demeanor might inspire you to take time away from others to reconnect with yourself.

As far as the art goes, the card is usually quite simple. An older man wanders through a dark and somber environment carrying a single lantern, providing himself with the only light he needs to explore and seek the answers he craves. I connect this card to throat chakra healing. By quieting distractions, we have the ability to draw our inner voice to the surface and hear from parts of ourselves that whisper sincere and profound truths. If you tend to identify as anxious or codependent in your friendships and community, this inward focus could feel uncomfortable or vulnerable. The word "hermit" might hold negative connotations, but this card is not meant to make you feel lonely. Let it inspire you to create respectful boundaries and protect your peace.

This is a card that suggests it's time to take that solo weekend trip or put your phone on silent. The cards are letting you know that being alone and completely in *your* energy could build a deeper knowing and trust within yourself. When you pull The Hermit, offer yourself a journey inward. I suggest you connect to your internal dialogue through meditation or journaling, as these practices can often provide more insight than a conversation with someone else.

Affirmation for The Hermit

"I see the value in stillness. I trust the voice I carry and honor it by resting it."

Connect to Your Story

Write about a time you first asked for advice from others but eventually came to your own conclusion by listening to your inner voice instead.

WHEEL of FORTUNE.

In My Story | Wheel of Fortune

Here it all comes,
A new life and new promises,
Throwing me toward paths I could have never
*   prepared for.*
I use my voice,
Not to object, simply to say thank you.

Keywords: Luck, Fate, Change, Destiny, Cycles, Misfortune, Release of control, Surrender

Element: Fire

Meaning

When the Wheel of Fortune card spins us (literally and energetically) in new directions, we begin to believe in something greater than ourselves. This card represents fate, destiny, good luck, and the closing and opening of new cycles, making it truly a wild card in the Major Arcana sequence. I see this card as a hint or clue from our Spirit Guides and the Universe, like a little bread crumb of confirmation that we're on the right track. There's something brewing for us behind the scenes. We can't yet access or understand its timing or details, but we can sense there's an energy of change around us. Spirit is plotting each synchronicity and serendipitous event for us, creating pathways we could've never imagined or planned for ourselves.

If you're reading this and it excites you, good! This card is a wonderful omen for aligned and destined opportunities to open up, but it requires us to release control and prepare for the unexpected.

The auspicious energy of the Wheel of Fortune revives our belief in fate and luck, so I recommend you lean into it. When we have been living in alignment with our higher self and greater purpose, honoring all our previous lessons, the Universe speeds up our timelines and rewards us with the expedited changes and shifts we've earned through our inner work.

You might notice that this energy feels very external when you pull it in a reading. It's like the Wheel of Fortune energy is happening *to* us rather than being consciously cocreated. This is because it's the midpoint in the Major Arcana cycle, and it's a chance for change to sweep through and spice things up. It's meant to feel out of our hands!

Affirmation for Wheel of Fortune

"I will allow change to rush in and take me where I am meant to be."

Connect to Your Story

In your journal, write about a time in your life when luck was on your side. How did this make you feel?

In My Story | Justice

The Universe will not fault you
Or punish you
For living your truth.

Keywords: Fairness, Truth, Law,
Justice or injustice, Cause and effect,
Decisions, Facts over feelings

Element: Air

Meaning

The Justice card demands fairness. Even keeled and unemotional, a leader (presumably a judge) holds balanced scales in his left hand. The strength of this card lies in the figure's definitive ability to make a choice and stick with it. After assessing and considering all the facts, this card gives us energy to decide, and once the case is closed, it's really closed.

The card brings up themes of truth, right versus wrong, and righteousness. It allows us to discern what feels moral and immoral and where energies need to be brought back into balance. This card could present itself when you're involved in any contractual agreement. Lawsuits, purchasing property, and divorce are all examples of this energy playing out in real life.

You could also notice that the Justice card feels quite formal—stuffy, even. It's similar to The Hierophant and The Emperor in that most readers find these controlled and intense energies inflexible. Remember that the Major Arcana is a series of lessons, teaching the young Fool how to be the best and most complete version of himself. In the Justice card energy, The Fool is learning that the truth sets us free and justice can (and hopefully does) prevail, but unfairness is part of our experience, too. What I enjoy about this theme is that it gives us a bit of a break from sifting through all the emotional and spiritual messages and brings a clarity that feels sharp, precise, and easily defined. We witness so many injustices day to day that this card can feel like it's pointing out where areas of our society, relationships, and experience are disproportionately unbalanced and unfair. I encourage you to sit with it and all that it stirs up. This illumination of injustices and wrongdoing can help clarify your responsibility to react or respond.

You'll notice in the Rider-Waite-Smith art that the judge wears red (a color of personal power) just like some of the other leaders in the Major Arcana, like The Hierophant and The Emperor. He is holding a sword pointed up at the heavens, a nod to the air element and the integrity this figure hopes to bring in by sharing the truth. Are you willing to be the judge and make fair and honest choices, assessments, and rulings for the greater good?

Affirmation for Justice
"I will view my life objectively, without harsh judgment."

Connect to Your Story
In your notebook, write about a time you experienced or witnessed injustice and how it affected you.

THE HANGED MAN.

In My Story | The Hanged Man
Sometimes the most subtle healing
Is the most substantial.

Keywords: Feeling stuck, Being in limbo, Exploring the gray area, Suspended in the unknown, Observation, New perspectives, Uncertainty, Lack of direction, Pause, Evolution, Questioning

Element: Water

Meaning
The Hanged Man speaks to that gray area we all find ourselves stuck in from time to time.

This card is our permission to pause just before we make any more moves when we are unsure how to proceed. At first glance, we might assume the character hanging by his toe is trying to get out of this compromising position right away. But the energy is more neutral than that; it's not a dire situation. Instead, he's relaxed! There's even a bright light circling around the crown of his head like a halo, indicating that he's receiving divine information. He is open for spiritual business, so to speak, although his body is limited right now.

When this card looms in front of us in a reading, it's instructing us to open our eyes and become more receptive to the subtle details that are going unnoticed. It supports us in gaining a new perspective first, then proceeding toward whatever new growth or movement we need once we are truly ready. This card is the opposite of some of the active and masculine energies we've already discussed in the Major Arcana cycle. The Hanged Man is using this in-between time to work on himself and find an energy that feels aligned and authentic. By flipping his perspective (quite literally upside down), he is able to see things with a different lens.

One of my favorite details in this card is the fact that the suspended figure is creating a shape similar to the number four with his legs. We've already learned in previous chapters that in tarot numerology the number four represents a time to pause, reflect, and slow down. As a reader, make note that this card can feel deeply uncomfortable or even triggering for some people you read for. Feeling stuck or trapped can be anxiety producing. Understand that this space is only temporary. While you wait, why not spend your time deepening your spiritual practice?

Affirmation for The Hanged Man

"I welcome stillness so I can notice the subtleties of my experience."

Connect to Your Story

With pen to paper, write about a time you were stuck in a "gray area" and what happened when you got unstuck.

In My Story | Death

(P)retending not
(T)o feel it all until finally
(S)urrendering to the label so I could
(D)iscover myself again.

Keywords: Destruction, Making room for something new, Transformation, Rebirth, Letting go, Healing, Endings, Closure, Soul alignment, Shedding old labels

Element: Water

Meaning

When the Death card arrives, we know a deep transformation is well underway. What appears to be a clear ending is simultaneously a beginning, and like many of the cycles in the tarot, there's a balance between shadow and light here. As we release and let go of something, we're equally met with the opportunity to expand. The Death card is about the physical release of something that no longer serves us. This can certainly be a relationship, a workplace environment, or a part of our rituals that are no longer in alignment with our growth. Saying goodbye is difficult, so while the decision to release could feel quite necessary, you're also allowed to mourn.

I like to remind my students that we've often had plenty of time to reflect on this ending. The card emphasizes physical release as our bodies shift away, but our hearts and minds have been prepared through the discerning Justice card and the patient Hanged Man themes prior.

Death is difficult due to its finality. When you pull this card, hold yourself in love and compassion. We've been programmed to believe that death is the absolute worst-case scenario. Without spiritually bypassing the discomfort of this ending, know that this card is truly focused on transformation and an opportunity to be reborn. It can signify an ego death and a chance for you as a reader to redefine and rediscover new parts of yourself with less influence from the past. I love the way the Rider-Waite-Smith depicts a corpse riding a horse, just like our knights in the Minor Arcana do. Since the knights are the movers and doers of the tarot, this imagery further drives home the message that what's done is done, and it's time to move forward and away, seeking and searching for experiences and opportunities that will be a better fit for your soul expansion.

Affirmation for Death

"I am willing to walk away from what doesn't serve me."

Connect to Your Story

Write about a chapter in your life when you were ready in your body and heart to leave something or someone behind.

In My Story | Temperance

What almost sunk you
Could become someone else's anchor.

Keywords: Balance, Healing, Moderation, Vulnerability, Softness, Patience, Calmness, Presence

Element: Fire

Meaning

After the unsettling experience of letting go in the Death card's energy, your nervous system might be longing to recalibrate and resettle. The Temperance card is just the relieving energy we need. This card represents balance, moderation, and coming back to a state of peace. There's a great deal of vulnerability and softness to this card as well, as our hearts could still feel raw and exposed from whatever we said goodbye to with Death. Temperance asks us to take care of ourselves. We must recreate and recommit to a lifestyle of moderation so we can sustain ourselves through the peaks and valleys that life throws our way.

Temperance is a card that has always resonated with me deeply. Balance isn't necessarily my strong suit (who's with me?), as it challenges us to surrender. If you, too, are someone who tends to thrive on doing *more*, searching for *more*, adding *more* to your plate, always looking externally for what *else* could be available to you, take this card as an invitation to make sustainable changes to your energy. Temperance encourages us to settle into what already exists within us and appreciate what we already have. This card supports our self-care and tells us that we have healing resources right at our fingertips.

In the traditional imagery, an angel rests at the water's edge with one foot in the water and one grounded on earth. Pouring water between two chalices, the angel is quite literally tempering the energy to soothe their emotions. My favorite part is how they're utilizing the healing power of water plus the grounding element of earth to take easy care of themselves, another example of this card's balance. If this card has chosen you in a reading, stop and consider what feels out of balance or disproportionate to your truest essence and alignment. How can you simplify your healing?

Affirmation for Temperance
"Balance will carry me further than chaos. Peace is my birthright."

Connect to Your Story
Write about a time in your life when you prioritized self-care, and consider how it affected your relationships, spirituality, and inner peace.

In My Story | The Devil

You are incredible,
Intoxicating,
Mesmerizing.

You are confusing,
Pitiful,
Frustrating.

Thank you for mirroring the most extreme
parts of me, too.

Keywords: Codependency, Addiction, Restriction, Lack of freedom, Unhealthy attachments, Shadow self, Toxic cycles

Element: Earth

Meaning

I don't like to sugarcoat The Devil. It's not meant to feel like an easy, breezy energy. This card has a low vibration, and it brings up difficult themes of codependency, addiction, and destructive, unhealthy patterns. We all have traits and tendencies that do not serve us, that become a crutch and a deterrent from our healing or potential. Devilish habits include overindulgence, doom scrolling on our phones, and people-pleasing. Occasionally, this card references abusive or addictive patterns or even deep-seated shameful cycles we are unaware of.

The Devil sheds light on the darker and uglier parts of the human experience. It can keep a tight grip on us, leaving us feeling out of control and powerless to a situation even though we have more freedom and sovereignty than we realize. Whether it's junk food or cheap thrills, our greed can get a taste of something and start craving more and more of it, even when it's not good for us.

The imagery usually mimics The Lovers card. This time, however, the independent characters are joined together under the forces of something less beautiful and bright, as an archangel is no longer hovering above them to gather them in union. Instead, the Devil chains the two parties together. Those shackles can energetically attach you to someone, something, or a shadow part of yourself.

The Devil indicates that there can always be too much of a good thing. The energy is gluttonous and greedy, ego-driven and hungry, overly sexualized or seeking constant stimulation. The Devil requires us to finally admit that while seeking control or power, we may have actually *lost* control or power. If the card holds you tightly in a reading, breathe; you have a conscious choice ahead of you. It's time to take an assessment of what in your life brings out the best in your energy and what makes you feel limited, driven by fear, or craving more chaos. If there are relationships that leave you feeling weak or small or habits you engage in like gossip or substances, are you willing to heal your dependency on them? This is one of the hardest, most liberating lessons The Fool will endure. You can and will find freedom, friend.

Affirmation for The Devil
"As I loosen my grip on control, I regain a hold on my life."

Connect to Your Story
Write about a time in your life when you were driven by greediness or power more than love and compassion. How did this affect your relationship with others and yourself?

In My Story | The Tower

She felt the world crumble beneath her,
Ungrounding.

This reckoning forced her to respond
By rising,

First out of survival,
Then out of grace.

Arriving far above the ashes in awe and
  appreciation for what she has previously
  destroyed,
And what had almost destroyed her.

Below her rested an earth that could not be shaken,
Moved, or disrupted anymore.

Keywords: Sudden change, Upheaval, Epiphanies, Destruction, Chaos, Uncomfortable transformation, Rebuilding foundations, Awakenings, Disasters, Loss

Element: Fire

Meaning

Here comes The Tower, stirring up some drama in your readings and cementing itself as possibly the most feared card in the deck. The Tower can trigger anxiety and fear because at its core, it's a card of destruction and epiphanies. The upheaval can make us uncomfortable because we are left in the ashes, forced to redirect ourselves and rebuild in ways we didn't plan on.

In the traditional imagery, we see a large and towering man-made structure that was built hastily. The creators cared less about the foundation and more about the tower standing the tallest and proudest, looking down at the earth that once held them. We watch as lightning hits The Tower, causing it to fall.

If you are in the midst of this type of change and restructuring in your life, I see you. The way this card dismantles energy is intense and startling, but you are just as intensely resilient and strong. The prior lesson in The Devil card might have been alluding to this potential event, pointing out the patterns that were reaching a breaking point and illuminating spaces in our experience that must change. Sometimes this card represents an internal epiphany or awakening, the sort of *aha* moment that makes us quickly pack our bags, move cities, quit jobs, or suddenly want out of a long-term relationship.

Without sounding like an irritating optimist, I want to assure you this revelation and destruction of ego-built energy will rock you, but also bring you closer to alignment. When the dust literally and figuratively settles, you might think to yourself, *It was for the best.*

There's something empowering about this Tower energy if we allow it to simply be. We face a choice: we can either resist and deny that this change is happening, or we can walk through the flames, excited to see what we can burn or destroy in the psyche and find ourselves safely resting on the other side of the ashes.

The good news is The Tower often burns quickly, intense for only a moment. Have compassion for yourself and others when it roars through a reading. The Tower requires us to surrender and shoves us toward the difficult lesson that sometimes change requires faith over fear.

Affirmation for The Tower
"I surrender as Spirit removes the obstacles that are not meant to be on my path."

Connect to Your Story
Reflect on and write about a time in your life when things had to fall apart to come back together.

In My Story | The Star

An exhale.

A chance to reimagine what's possible when
I'm not running from challenges or fueled
by grief.

A sweeping inhale that soothes me rather than
shrinks the magic housed in my heart.

A time to fill the body with life and love,
simple love.

A time to use my sovereign strength and deepest
knowing to direct and guide me.

A time where quiet has finally rolled over to
replace the thunder, a peaceful settling.

An exhale,
Followed by a loving inhale.
An exhale,
Followed by a healing inhale.

Keywords: Renewed hope, Recommitment to faith, Finding purpose, Vulnerability, Spirituality, Wish fulfillment

Element: Air

Meaning

The Star card is a breath of fresh air. But before I share why, may I remind you of who you were at the beginning of this journey? The Fool (you) was once uninfluenced and naïve, filled with optimism and an eagerness to learn. Since then, you've endured plenty of lessons. To put it frankly, you've been "going through it" in the recent Major Arcana events, meeting some of the uglier energies of the deck. But now The Star card is glimmering above you, offering faith, hope, and what might feel like a windfall of apologies from Spirit. The Star has a sincere energy, giving us space to finally exhale. We've just overcome a series of rocky hardships, and now we have an opportunity to make peace with our stories thus far.

In the Rider-Waite-Smith deck, there is a figure who's brought to their knees, resting by the water's edge. Similar to the Temperance card, they are using this time to rejuvenate themselves. In this card they're also naked, appearing vulnerable and exposed but choosing to find rest and comfort regardless. The Star card is sometimes referred to as the wish fulfillment card because it offers the opportunity for fateful and destined wishes to finally come true. I consider this card to be a very healing, incredibly comforting, and a card that we should celebrate each time we see it in a reading.

The Star also helps us better understand what makes us truly special, like the stars we admire on a clear evening. A spiritual archetype, The Star is a fantastic card to pull if you're looking to awaken or enrich your spiritual or psychic connection. When you draw it from the deck, rest in gratitude for a breath or two. This is a beautiful space to be. You're held by your faith, so know that your spirit guides are taking care of the rest.

Affirmation for The Star

"My struggles shaped me, and moving forward I will lead with
love, purpose, and faith."

Connect to Your Story

In your journal, write and reflect on a time when the stars felt aligned for you. How did it feel to be held by the Universe?

In My Story | The Moon

Even the strongest people have experienced
that swell of emotion
That seems to only show up at night.

It's as if the sun knows
That we prefer not to be seen when
we surrender.

Keywords: Secrecy, Illusion, Shadow, Fear, Anxiety, Subconscious connection, Intuition

Element: Water

Meaning

The Moon is a card of mystery, and like anything that's unknown, it can make us feel left in the dark. There's something so daunting about its energy, like we could be swallowed whole by the capacity of its fullness. But I'd like to remind you that it's in the exploration of the dark that we can find depth and meaning in our inner landscapes.

Emotions can run incredibly high when The Moon appears. Just like the ocean is influenced by its phases, so are we. Similar to the energy of The High Priestess, who also channels beautiful lunar light, we have an opportunity here to dive into the depths of the psyche and explore the subconscious in new and intimate ways. This card has the ability to lift a veil and bring us closer to our intuitive power as well. The Moon says, "Admire me. Do not resist or fear the fullness of these feelings or the imperfection of each of your phases."

Highly emotional, intuitive, and healing, this card is asking that you look *deeper* and break through any facades you could be using to cover your true expression. This card offers us another way of putting our intuition into practice and *listening* to the cues of the Universe rather than immediately judging them or yourself. I joke sometimes that this card can indicate the third eye is a little *too* open. As our intuition blossoms, our psychic senses can feel like they're in overdrive, so be sure to balance all this feminine power with grounding practices that keep you in your body as you explore the depths of your subconscious connection. Dawn will break and appear again, and we will be enveloped in light soon, so while we're here in the dark, why not explore and dance in the shadows?

Affirmation for The Moon

"The darkness I find when I close my eyes can feel as nourishing as the warmth of the sun."

Connect to Your Story

Write about a time where your intuition felt so accurate it overwhelmed you.

In My Story | The Sun

There's so much light
Available to me,
It's almost blinding.

Keywords: Positivity, Fun, Success, Optimism, Vitality, Sincerity, Warmth, Joy

Element: Fire

Meaning

The Sun card asks us to bask in our divine light for a moment (or hopefully far longer). This card exudes confidence, self-assurance, and playfulness. It's perhaps the highest vibrational energy in the deck, and it usually symbolizes successes, victories, and experiences that fill us to the very brim with happiness. When it appears in a reading, it feels like the ultimate confirmation. I teach my tarot students to use this card as a stamp of approval. It's the tarot's way of saying, "Hell yes!" in response to whatever question we asked or area we are seeking clarity on. The Sun supports and spotlights whatever you're doing and offers encouragement because you're doing it well and with authenticity.

This card asks us to be present and enjoy the ride of life, and it's through The Sun's optimism and joy that we can feel magnetic and seen. I recommend you savor these good times while they're available. Speaking of the ride of life, the art of this card quite literally shows that. A young cherub sits joyfully on horseback, along for the journey. What I find so beautiful about The Sun card is that it implies The Fool has regressed back to a playful and childlike essence. As we get closer and closer to completing the cycle of the Major Arcana, it's warming and wonderful to see The Fool enjoy the simple pleasures of light, laughter, and play.

Having witnessed and moved through many seasons of difficulty at this point, we start to appreciate these beautiful moments with a sense of all-encompassing gratitude. Enjoy yourself! If this card is shining on you in a reading, I encourage you to lift your gaze and admire the beauty in your life. After all, it reflects your inner warmth.

Affirmation for The Sun

"I attract the most success when I let joy lead me."

Connect to Your Story

Recall the memory and sit with it first, then write about a time when you felt truly joyful and vibrant.

In My Story | Judgement

I hear my guides say,
"There is nothing you could have done
*   differently."*
And after months of agonizing over the details,
Forgiveness replaced my guilt.

Keywords: Rebirth, Forgiveness, Judgement, Releasing guilt, A declaration, Introspection

Element: Fire

Meaning

Judgement gives us the opportunity to rewrite our narrative, let go of the heaviness, and forgive ourselves for our imperfections (no easy feat). It also brings forth epiphanies and awakenings, and can lead us to realizations around our purpose or push us toward spiritual expansion. Over the course of the Major Arcana cycle, you've been learning not only about yourself, but about your relationship and dynamic with Spirit overall. You are here on Earth for a reason, and figuring out what the Universe is asking of you can take a few (or more) cycles as you learn new aspects of yourself in each.

If your head is spinning a bit from the complexity of this card, I hear ya. If I had to choose a card that remains the most naggingly difficult for me, it's this one. I encourage you to think about the tarot at large for a moment. The Fool's journey is meant to represent a life cycle, and we might not have reached a state of complete forgiveness or found our soul calling at the time of pulling this card, but that's okay. Rather than labeling or placing specific judgments on the actions you've taken and the choices you've made, I suggest you process all your failures and regrets as sacred information that is necessary to help you reconnect and align with your highest self.

Take note of how the Judgement card comes out of nowhere, unprompted by any chaos or difficulty. We were previously riding the high of The Sun and feeling unstoppable, and it's at this point that we're left with one more deep and complex energy to process. Judgement is the self-reflection and deep inner work we *choose* to do.

Affirmation for Judgement
  "I forgive and surrender to my inner calling."

Connect to Your Story
Write about a time you chose forgiveness in order to feel more free.

THE WORLD.

In My Story | The World
"Thank you for never giving up on me,"
I said.

"You're very welcome,"
I replied.

Keywords: Completion, Wholeness, Achievement, Closure, Desired outcomes, Holistic happiness, Enlightenment, Ability to see the big picture

Element: Earth

Meaning
Filled with satisfaction and purpose, The World is a card of oneness, an energy we can tap into when we feel truly content and aligned with the boldest, richest version of ourselves. If you are feeling this sense of self-connection, know that you arrived in this full state because you've been consciously taking care of yourself!!

While this card can feel similar to the successes and celebrations of other cards, like The Sun, the satisfaction of The World feels more holistic to me. It typically represents that we have found ease in all areas of our lives: our relationships are healthy and strong, we're rooted in purpose, and we spend our time in ways that nourish us. It's a type of happiness that extends across all parts of our world. This is the grand finale of the Major Arcana, and your Spirit Guides are offering a round of applause. You've listened to and answered the call of your higher self.

Like all the endings in the tarot, our experience never completely crosses the finish line. Endings and closures open new doors and allow us to redefine ourselves once more. I think my absolute favorite detail that Pamela Colman Smith added to the traditional deck was the large wreath around the figure's body. Wreaths are seen as celebratory in the tarot (we see one depicted in the Six of Wands as well), and this wreath is huge, creating a perfect oval shape around their body. The detail takes on new meaning when we realize it's creating The Fool's number: zero. There's an opportunity to start the entire cycle over again, unnumbered and unafraid, should you choose to.

Sometimes readers will interpret this card as an opportunity to travel, explore new lands, and seek more growth. It's like we have an opportunity to take our completeness and confidence to new spaces, cultures, and experiences for the sake of sharing as well as learning more about what The World has to offer to us.

Perhaps you've pulled this card and are not feeling particularly harmonious or satisfied in this moment, and if that's the case, remain patient and keep holding the vision. Validate yourself and know that the small and incremental steps you are taking are creating a world you're going to be proud to occupy. This card is the perfect example of how prioritizing ourselves can lead to great satisfaction and success, and that the inner work is certainly worth it.

Affirmation for The World

"I am whole. I was always whole."

Connect to Your Story

Write about a time in your life when you had a lot to be grateful for. Then, sit in the present and notice how many of those gifts are still around you.

Conclusion

While writing this book, I hosted a retreat with twelve of my closest clients in the desert of Joshua Tree. I questioned myself, wondering if it was idiotic to spend my energy creating a healing container for others when my first manuscript deadline was just a month away.

I *should* have been writing, but I'm so grateful I listened to my intuition when it told me to host the retreat anyway. It must have sensed that this retreat would be exactly what I needed: a creative push to the end of this project. That weekend remains one of the most rewarding memories I have as a tarot reader. It was incredible to lead it in tandem with the writing process, knowing I was working to share and build a book that could reach far more than those twelve souls. I even read snippets and passages of the book to my guests, letting them in on the secret "behind the scenes," because they cocreated this book with me in many ways. I often compare the cards to mirrors, as they reflect our potential, but these women are my mirrors as well.

The women who attended this retreat have worked with me for years and learned the tarot alongside me through my online classes and training. Because they turned to me for personal readings over the course of their own healing journeys, I knew their stories as well as I knew my own. I'm honored to have had that close of a connection to each of them—not to mention a front row seat to marvel at their growth. They deeply inspire me and absolutely inspired *The Inner Tarot*.

At many points throughout our long weekend together, I'd glance around the home we were sharing and witness them cleansing their decks or discussing a symbol in a card. I'd watch as one group member conducted a reading for another. I eavesdropped on some of the most beautiful and authentic conversations while an overwhelming sense of gratitude left me with full-body chills. There were moments where I'd chuckle, noticing my direct influence in their card descriptions as they regurgitated words and metaphors I've used to describe the cards many times. I can promise you've read those words and phrases yourself as you conclude this book.

On the retreat there was plenty of tarot practice, but there were also nights around the fire where we laughed until we cried. We never had to cover or apologize for our tears. We told secrets, made discoveries about ourselves, and encouraged each other to challenge our inner healing practices, sometimes with cards in our hands, and other times with nothing but our hearts. On that trip we *lived* our tarot.

As you continue your practice as a tarot reader and intuitive, imagine yourself with us in that cozy cocoon of community. Each of us is on an individual journey toward transformation, yes, but we're never truly alone. And while I can't promise to lead a retreat with every one of my readers (although how freakin' cool would that be?), I assure you that the intention of this book is to remain congruent with what inspired those gatherings in the first place.

My hope is that you also get the opportunity to live your tarot and make this practice your own. I dream that you drop the "shoulds" and expose your most beautiful secrets to yourself and those you deem worthy enough to hear them. I encourage you to question, challenge, then ignore those who mock this practice. Develop a loving and open relationship with your gifts, your intuition, the cards, and the infinite magic within you. Feel free to explore this modality with confidence and share it with others. When you sit down to tap into your sacred ritual for readings, I hope you can feel the encouragement of a community much bigger than you at your back.

Through each shuffle and surrender to the messages, we collectively embrace and embody The Fool, building upon our lives through trial and error and slowly creating The World we are proud to rest within.

While I can't eavesdrop on your card interpretations or read your channeled writing, trust that I see, appreciate, and honor the parts of you that healed while sharing them. Let us now heal on behalf of those who came before us, those who are among us, and the souls we have yet to meet, including the versions of ourselves we may encounter along the journey.

Thank you, reader and now friend.

Acknowledgments

Throughout the creation of this book, I felt a tremendous amount of support from many souls. It is with immense gratitude that I offer my thanks to those who helped me channel this book and bring it to life.

To my tarot students and loyal community: I cannot find the words to express my appreciation for you. Thank you for taking part in my greatest joy of sharing these cards. Your stories are represented in these pages alongside my own, and our studies together guided the creation and manifestation of this book. I hope I've made you all proud.

To my teachers and mentors: There are those of you who directly impacted and witnessed my growth and others who guided my work and exploration of intuition from a distance. You are all sacred to me.

To Kelly Bergh: Thank you for working with me to create a proposal I could present to publishers and my agent with pride. What started with a tarot reading led to the best investment I've ever made in my business and has grown to become a friendship I cherish. Here's to many girls' trips, yoga flows, and afternoons spent writing together.

To Leigh Eisenman, my literary agent: You calmed my nerves and always had reassuring answers while bringing warmth and excitement to the experience of selling my book and becoming a first-time author. I'm so grateful to have you on my team.

To Diana Ventimiglia and Lyric Dodson, my editors at Sounds True: Your immediate enthusiasm and belief in my work gave me instant confirmation that my book was going to be in the very best hands. I can't thank you enough for believing so deeply in my vision and this project.

To Liz Moody and Lindsay Grimes: Thank you, Liz, for validating my desire to write and giving me the push to get started, and thank you, Lindsay, for offering to make a kismet introduction to our agent. You two are fellow authors I admire and friends who offered the gentle (but necessary) nudge to steer me closer toward my dream. This journey would have looked profoundly different without your generosity.

To Alexa Sharwell: My friend and ally on my team as I wrote this book, you held my business with the same love and care that I do. Thank you for being someone I could turn to and trust as I balanced this project with other endeavors.

To Lauren O'Connell and Angelica Ray: My friends, you are two incredible intuitive readers. Your accuracy in predicting this publishing journey astounds me. You both helped prepare me for the most exciting process of my professional life and the whirlwind of selling a book.

To Michelle Azzi: You are a talented and brilliantly creative designer. Thank you for supporting the design of the book cover in the beginning stages. Your magic helped bring my vision to life.

To my mother: We have healed together in countless ways and, I believe, in many lifetimes. Our closeness is something I cherish and never take for granted. Thank you for encouraging my creativity, femininity, and power, and for helping me create the life of my dreams. I am your Jo March, and you are my Marmee.

To my father: You have been proud of me during my darkest moments and for my brightest successes. I hope you know the way you look at me with awe does not go unnoticed. Thank you for never giving up on my healing process and being my biggest fan.

To my grandmothers and great grandmothers: You are a part of my lineage, my story, my feminine expression. I am *me* because of each of you. You are all magic.

To my grandfather: You bring so much laughter to my life. Laughter heals, and I hope you know some of my favorite silly moments have been with you.

To my late friend Teddy: I can always feel you in spirit. Thank you for being one of my first guides. You confirmed a gift I might never have trusted by reminding me that my path was destined all along.

To my closest friends and soul sisters: While we may not be connected by blood, I feel surrounded by your support and generosity every moment of every day. Friendship is such a gift. I am blessed to love, witness, and grow beside some of the strongest women in the world. You are absolutely my family.

And to my beloved partner, Kameron: Thank you for being the kindest, most loving and understanding person in my life. You are my safe space and my favorite soul to sit beside at a coffee shop on any morning. We were naïve and young Fools once, but our paths and lessons led us back to each other. You remain my proof that fate must be real. Our love is sincere and endless, and your approach to life has inspired me in many ways while on this journey of becoming an author. Thank you for being a proofreader, photographer, and morale booster every step of the way. You are my Two of Cups to Ten of Cups, and I'm so honored that bits of our love story will live on the pages of this book forever.

Notes

Chapter 1: In Review: The History of Tarot

1. Jessica Hundley, *Tarot* (Cologne: Taschen, 2020), 10–19.
2. Tim Husband, "Before Fortune-Telling: The History and Structure of Tarot Cards," *In Season* (blog), April 8, 2016, metmuseum.org /blogs/in-season/2016/tarot.
3. Hundley, *Tarot,* 20–35.
4. Benebell Wen, *Holistic Tarot: An Integrative Approach to Using Tarot for Personal Growth* (Berkeley, CA: North Atlantic Books, 2015), 7–11.
5. David Parlett, "tarot," Encyclopedia Britannica, December 12, 2022, britannica.com/topic/tarot; Husband, "Before Fortune-Telling."
6. Hundley, *Tarot,* 10–19.
7. Husband, "Before Fortune-Telling"; Hundley, *Tarot,* 10–19.
8. Hundley, *Tarot,* 10–19.
9. Parlett, "tarot."
10. Hundley, *Tarot,* 10–19.
11. Hundley, *Tarot,* 10–19.
12. Hundley, *Tarot,* 20–35.
13. Jacqui Palumbo, "The Woman Behind the World's Most Famous Tarot Deck Was Nearly Lost in History," CNN, May 12, 2022, cnn.com/style/article/pamela-colman-smith-tarot-art-whitney /index.html.
14. Wen, *Holistic Tarot,* 7–11.

About the Author

Kate Van Horn is a tarot reader, psychic, and spiritual mentor. She is a 500-hour Registered Yoga Teacher and a certified intuitive healer. She is the creator of (in) a healing space, a virtual community and membership committed to inner healing and intuitive work. She offers one-on-one readings to clients internationally as well as online courses teaching others how to read tarot and engage in channeled writing.

As a mental health advocate and trauma survivor, Kate credits her intuitive gifts and psychic abilities to life experience and difficult traumas. She candidly speaks about these chapters of her life and shares her path to healing in hopes of inspiring others to radically accept their stories, bodies, and gifts. She believes tarot can be an important tool for self-transformation and serve as a beautiful complement to holistic healing. Kate lives with her partner in Hermosa Beach, CA. This is her first book.

About Sounds True

Sounds True was founded in 1985 by Tami Simon with a clear mission: to disseminate spiritual wisdom. Since starting out as a project with one woman and her tape recorder, we have grown into a multimedia publishing company with a catalog of more than 3,000 titles by some of the leading teachers and visionaries of our time, and an ever-expanding family of beloved customers from across the world.

In more than three decades of evolution, Sounds True has maintained our focus on our overriding purpose and mission: to wake up the world. We offer books, audio programs, online learning experiences, and in-person events to support your personal growth and awakening, and to unlock our greatest human capacities to love and serve.

At SoundsTrue.com you'll find a wealth of resources to enrich your journey, including our weekly *Insights at the Edge* podcast, free downloads, and information about our nonprofit Sounds True Foundation, where we strive to remove financial barriers to the materials we publish through scholarships and donations worldwide.

To learn more, please visit SoundsTrue.com/freegifts or call us toll-free at 800.333.9185.

Together, we can wake up the world.